WOMAN PISSING

WOMAN

PISSING

Elizabeth Cooperman

UNIVERSITY OF NEBRASKA PRESS   *Lincoln*

Library of Congress Control
Number: 2021060192

Set in Adobe Text by Mikala R. Kolander.
Designed by N. Putens.

For M and D, my benevolent creators.

And in memory of H, artist.

All of writing is a huge lake.
There are great rivers that
feed the lake, like Tolstoy and
Dostoevsky. And there are
trickles, like Jean Rhys.

—JEAN RHYS

How unbearable it would be to
die—to leave "scraps," "bits," . . .
nothing really finished.

—KATHERINE MANSFIELD

I start with a blank, and there's
nothing more *horrifying* than a
blank canvas, 'cause I don't have
a thought or idea . . .

—LEE KRASNER

The flawed premise of this book humiliates me as much as the flawed execution. I tried starting with God, Picasso, my mother, springtime, etc., and nothing jelled. With each new beginning, the project collapsed in another way.

Not that problems like these are interesting, or even unique. Not that I think the way I am starting now is acceptable either. Everyone knows it's tacky for a writer to point at her seams, her hems, the green underpainting or dead layer of her canvas.

To my horror, a friend read a draft of this book and said it took about forty pages to settle in. So I decided to include the following diagrams as a way to stall the opening of the book. I thought the diagrams might distract from the dryness of the beginning chapters, which that same reader also compared to stale banana bread.

I showed the diagrams to another friend who unfortunately found them weak and not very interesting. I had drafted them in the first place as a way to think through some of the themes of the book while putting off the actual writing of the book.

It's clear to me now that nothing can save us from the crisis of beginning.

Create:

TO father bring forth multiply beget breed
enact coin hatch yield originate actualize
evoke   produce through effort   make cause
bubble smelt arouse stir draw forth style
bring to being engender procreate render
realize give rise to work substantiate
clear a path by removing objects for   conjure
sire confect paint intertwine turn out give
tack together components develop   mother

Night

TO father bring forth multiply beget breed
enact coin hatch yield originate actualize
evoke   produce through effort make cause
bubble smelt arouse stir draw forth style
bring to being engender procreate render
realize give rise to work substantiate
clear a path by removing objects for   conjure
sire confect paint intertwine turn out give
tack together components develop   mother

Day

Night

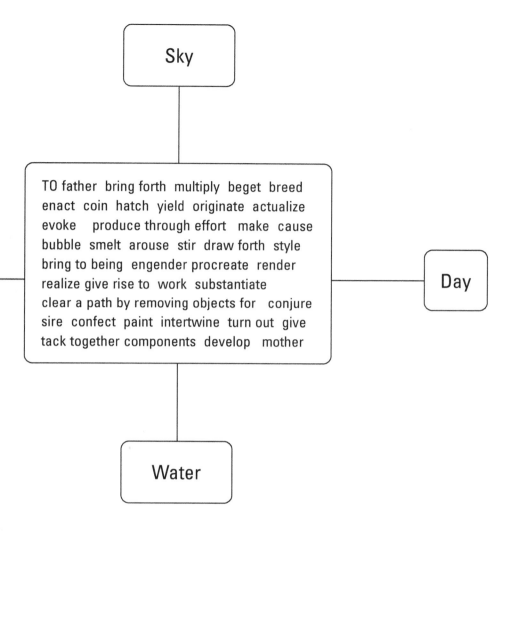

Sky

TO father bring forth multiply beget breed
enact coin hatch yield originate actualize
evoke   produce through effort make cause
bubble smelt arouse stir draw forth style
bring to being engender procreate render
realize give rise to work substantiate
clear a path by removing objects for   conjure
sire confect paint intertwine turn out give
tack together components develop   mother

Day

Water

Night

Sky

TO father bring forth multiply beget breed
enact coin hatch yield originate actualize
evoke   produce through effort make cause
bubble smelt arouse stir draw forth style
bring to being engender procreate render
realize give rise to work substantiate
clear a path by removing objects for   conjure
sire confect paint intertwine turn out give
tack together components develop   mother

Day

Earth / Dry Land

Seas

"Let the earth sprout vegetation"

Seed-bearing plants

Fruit trees of every kind on earth that bear fruit with the seed in it

xxx Stars xxxxx

Moon

Night

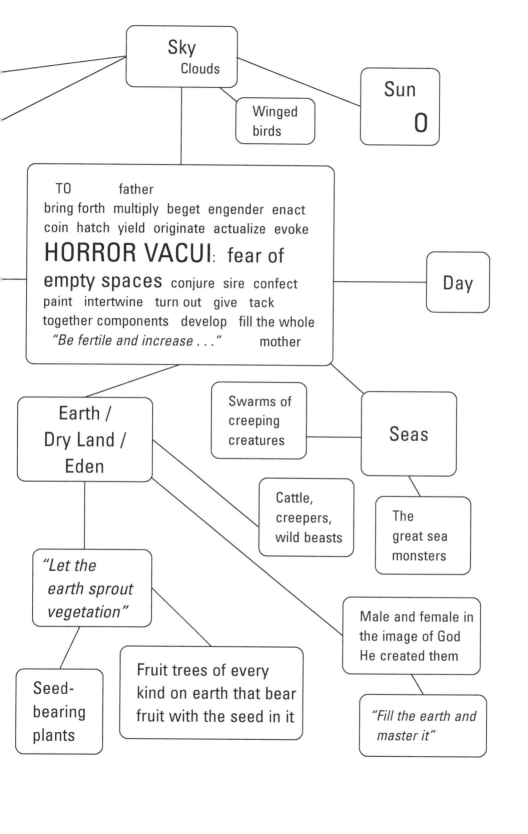

Sky
Clouds

Sun
0

Winged
birds

TO   father
bring forth multiply beget engender enact
coin hatch yield originate actualize evoke
HORROR VACUI: fear of
empty spaces conjure sire confect
paint intertwine turn out give tack
together components develop fill the whole
"Be fertile and increase . . ."   mother

Day

Earth /
Dry Land /
Eden

Swarms of
creeping
creatures

Seas

Cattle,
creepers,
wild beasts

The
great sea
monsters

*"Let the
earth sprout
vegetation"*

Male and female in
the image of God
He created them

Seed-
bearing
plants

Fruit trees of every
kind on earth that bear
fruit with the seed in it

*"Fill the earth and
master it"*

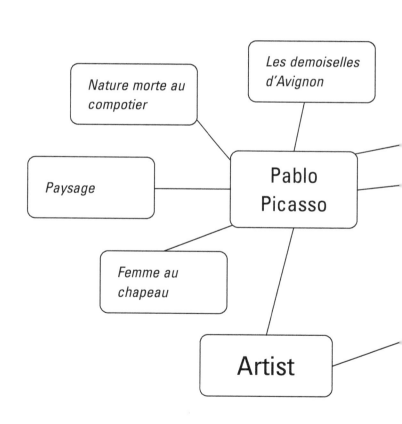

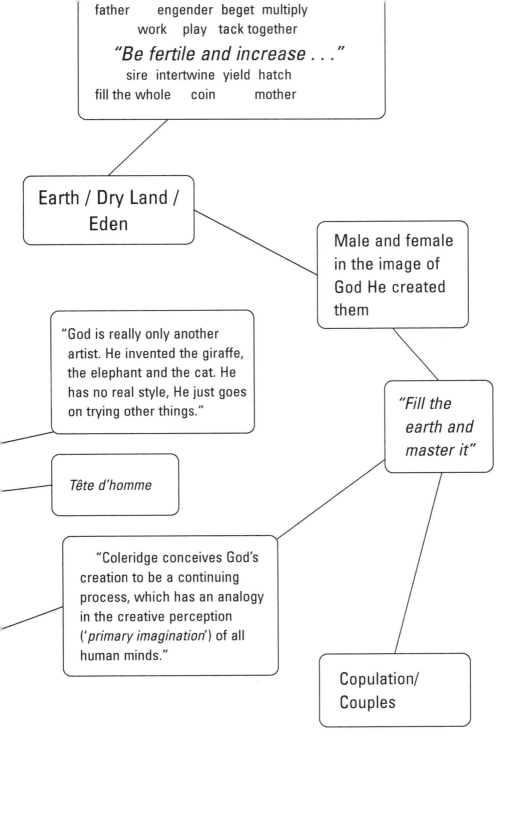

father   engender beget multiply
work   play   tack together

"Be fertile and increase . . ."

sire intertwine yield hatch
fill the whole   coin   mother

Earth / Dry Land / Eden

Male and female in the image of God He created them

"God is really only another artist. He invented the giraffe, the elephant and the cat. He has no real style, He just goes on trying other things."

"Fill the earth and master it"

Tête d'homme

"Coleridge conceives God's creation to be a continuing process, which has an analogy in the creative perception (*'primary imagination'*) of all human minds."

Copulation/ Couples

"My mother said to me, if you are a soldier, you will become a general. If you are a monk, you will become the Pope. Instead I was a painter, and became Picasso."

"All art is erotic."

"You have to know how to be vulgar. Paint with four-letter words."

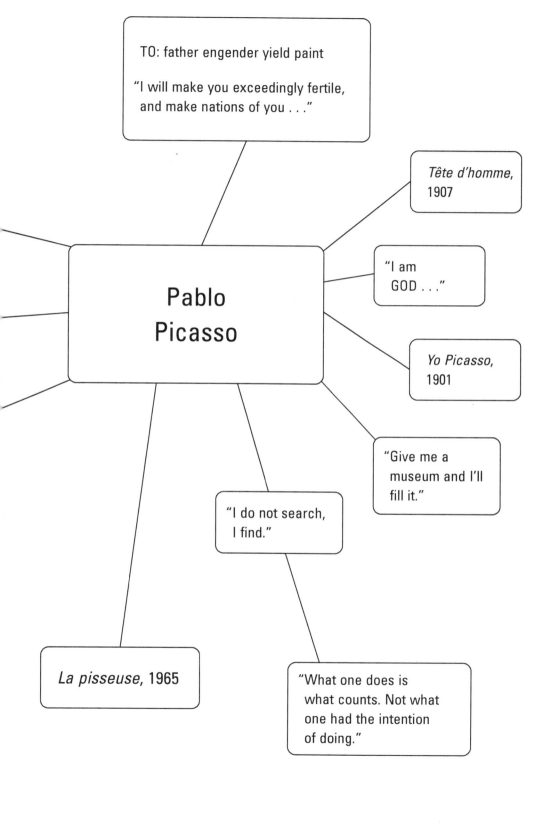

TO: father engender yield paint

"I will make you exceedingly fertile,
and make nations of you . . ."

Pablo
Picasso

Tête d'homme,
1907

"I am
GOD . . ."

Yo Picasso,
1901

"Give me a
museum and I'll
fill it."

"I do not search,
I find."

La pisseuse, 1965

"What one does is
what counts. Not what
one had the intention
of doing."

Picasso

La pisseuse, 1965

WOMAN PISSING

Woman with Hat

My friend Vedika, a zany painter in her sixties, told me that when she was young, she tore up all the quotes from writers she used to love and vowed to follow her own wisdom. Don't listen to those preachers 'cause they're just mammals like you, she said.

I've come to realize that I'm too susceptible to everyone else's philosophies, which is why I doubt my own wisdom, which is why I found Vedika's story, too, so attractive.

Good writing seems to come from good taste. Sometimes I think that's all there is to it. So many people I know, especially artists, luxuriate in the finicky nature of their taste. They enjoy their response to stimuli and trust that response. But I have never understood (possessed) taste—in music, in wine, in clothes, in home decorating.

Even a child, whether she loves ABBA or clarinet, seems more confident in her aesthetic.

I had hoped to invent a literary form that could accommodate ambivalence, hesitation, crippling self-doubt, lack of any sense of the way forward.

Idea: compose the whole book as a showcase of my attempts to write the first paragraph of the book. (Someone has probably used that trick before.)

The Artist recommends a book of essays. He found it slow, boring, and nebulous—says, I think you'd like it.

When I was an infant, my mom took me to the doctor to report a sinus infection. She doesn't have sinuses yet, said the doctor. When my mom brought me back, the doctor looked again and admitted her mistake— that indeed I had full-blown sinusitis. My mom theorizes this may have wrecked my sense of smell, and I wonder now if (along with smell) taste, desire, and aversion also flew out the window—if this mishap accounts for my artistic problems.

I'm always reinventing myself, says the Artist, and I don't think you are.

He says to captivate him I'd have to wear a different hat every day.

Head of a Man

To human beings, said Coleridge, God gave a creative imagination resembling his own. "God is just another Artist like me," said Picasso, audaciously flipping the narrative. "I am God. I am God. I am God." He, too, could make Day and Night, Countryside and Seaside, She-Goat and Dove. He could make *Tête d'homme* or *Head of a Woman* to his heart's content.

As a young man, Picasso imitated sculptures from antiquity, endowing his figures with huge eyes, huge lips, and thick fingers.

Maybe it felt like he could double himself through this gigantic style, multiply his strength even beyond God's: "He was a very short man and he had a great respect for gigantism," said biographer John Richardson.

Picasso delighted in spectacles like the circus, the imagination writ large. In 1917 he designed the stage set, costumes, and theater curtain for the first cubist ballet, *Parade*, about a troupe of circus performers that try to seduce pedestrians on a Paris boulevard into their circus tent, where a show is about to begin. To fashion cubist costumes and props, Picasso worked fluently with sculptural materials—wood, metal, papier-mâché, cloth—and also body paint. On the athletic legs of the acrobat Lydia Lopoukhova, he hand-painted spiral designs.

Like Picasso, the word *parade* comes from the French via the Spanish (*parada*, "a stopping place"). And as if on parade, the apple, the actor, the blind man, the chanteuse, the nanny goat, the woman with a feathered hat, the Spanish woman, the pregnant woman, the sick woman, the beggar, all marched through Picasso's imagination. He could juggle and endlessly recast the world through paint, metal, stone, clay, wax, wood, scrap material. "An artist's calling," says George Kubler, "is to evoke a perpetual renewal of form in matter." He is *homo faber*: "Man the Maker," "Man the Smith."

It's ironic to me that Coleridge likened an artist's imagination to some movie projection of God's, considering that Coleridge himself became so frustrated with his creative weaknesses that he abandoned poetry altogether, confessing he had "a smack of Hamlet" in him. He thought himself better suited to writing criticism. (Ironically, says one editor, his poetry lives on whereas today we rarely read the criticism at all.)

In the Old Testament story of Genesis, what interests me is that God has a sort of split personality. During the first seven days, his work pleases him. He congratulates himself and rests on his laurels. He is Picassian. Later, though, a frustrated God changes his mind and sets out to destroy the artworks he once loved.

Head of a Woman

Lee Krasner remembers that one day she walked into a studio space hung floor to ceiling with her drawings and "hated it all, took it down, tore everything and threw it on the floor."

She began as Lena Krassner. Sometimes she signed her name Lenore, Lee, or LK. She felt antsy in her name.

Born in Brooklyn to immigrant parents who worked as humble fishmongers and spoke little English, Lee loved to read, though was probably dyslexic.

Much has been made of Lee's looks, probably because she came of age in a macho art scene. She had a sexy, compact body but gawky facial features—a large Jewish nose—what some even called an ugly face. As most female artists did at the time, she modeled for other artists. A photographer who frequently sought her out liked her most as a hand model.

As a student, Krasner struggled with art and lacked confidence in her abilities. "The only reason I'm passing you in art," said her high school teacher, "is because you've done so excellently in all your other subjects." At the Women's Art division of Cooper Union, where most women prepared for careers in the fashion industry or interior design, the life drawing teacher chastised Krasner repeatedly: "I can't do anything with you," he sighed.

One summer she slaved over a self-portrait *en plein aire*. "It was difficult," she remembered, "the light in the mirror, the heat, the bugs." She painted herself in the act of painting, wearing a masculine blue work shirt and dirty artist's smock. The top corner of the canvas mistakenly tips toward Krasner's head instead of away, as if it might fall off the easel. She does not smirk or wink. "I am preoccupied with trying to know myself in order to communicate with others."

Parisian painters were all the rage in the States when Krasner was coming up, especially Picasso and Matisse, and she began using Picasso's cloisonné style, outlining shapes in a thick black line and incorporating large areas of "pure" color into her increasingly abstract compositions, "but unlike Picasso she built up heavily encrusted surfaces."

An overworked surface—an impasto too thick—can look, as I know all too well, dry as an old piece of bread, or crusty as a scab.

"[Picasso] had few creative problems," writes biographer Pierre Cabanne, "and was not really interested in their solutions. Even if he had some technical difficulties in developing his medium, it was not a major worry; one thing was worth another." Meanwhile Krasner often worked from a vexed place: "It takes enormous energy to keep growing," she said of her process, "and it is painful."

Picasso to Tériade, 1923: How many times, going for blue, I found I didn't have any. So I used red instead.

Krasner to God: Yellow is an extremely difficult color. I don't know why.

Why do I get stuck in a process that other people flow joyfully through? I think I get caught on my reflection, caught looking at myself, reviling myself.

Diarists I admire: Hejinian, Connolly, Julavits, Gornick, Ernaux, Markson. Have I learned nothing at all from them?

Self-doubt probably has to do with a fear of looking bad—with a sort of anxiety about self-disclosure.

My writing self seems to tap into the lowest part of my personality—the critic, the misanthrope, the small part, the weak part, the jealous part, the insecure part, the doubting Debbie—whereas I get the sense that for some people making art expands them, uplifts them, makes them greater, more generous, more able to love, and ultimately more divine. At least on the page or the canvas.

Tibetan monk Chögyam Trungpa says if you make art like someone constipated on a toilet seat, it will be "meek" and overly "technical." The constipated artist will refer back to technicalities and not feel happy about the whole.

Woman with Green Stockings

Many young, lonely women living in cities have their year of black-and-white photography. During my year, I documented a group of trees in my neighborhood that arched in a long, sharp line toward the lake. I couldn't resist taking those photos in full sun, despite knowing I'd overexpose the film.

The only photographs that came out in the darkroom that year came from an indoor series I took in my depressing, windowless bathroom, where I happened to be hand-washing lingerie: several pairs of black, navy, and teal stockings floating in a soapy bath in the sink. In this bath, the stockings expanded into abstract shapes.

Even though the photographs are unlikable and I've never showed them to anyone, I found the images surprising and wondered from what source genius springs. Are acts of genius just accidents, I wondered, or whispered into ears by the muse.

In photography, painting, and poetry alike, I get the sense that the muses never so much abandoned me as brushed right past, like posh gallery-goers unmoved by yet another canvas. Unknowingly, have I been brazen, insubordinate in the muses' eyes?

I guess you could consider this one long complaint to the museum of thwarted inspiration.

Crouching Beggar

At ninety-three the Old Blind Man is still waiting to get published in the *New York Times* or picked up by some prestigious publishing house. Under the bed he stores a large red box of his poems and stories, mostly about the desert, the ocean, the people he's met riding the train, or famous writers he's observed like zoo animals at summer writing conferences.

But for now he and I have a bond: we are the number one fanboy and fangirl of what we call real artists. The Old Blind Man loves to philosophize about what defines an artist, what defines a writer: an artist is born not made; an artist is more creative when he's alone and suffering a little bit; an artist should only marry someone who understands that artists need to be free; you can recognize an artist by his hands or by his burning eyes; a writer should be truthful like a child; a poet is someone whose head goes round and round in circles. Great writers sublimate, says the Old Blind Man. That's art! If you're happily married and have sex, you don't have to write a damn thing.

Stephen Crane wrote *The Red Badge of Courage* because his fingers itched, the Old Blind Man explains to me, and Rachmaninoff had enormous hands—he could play tremendous chords. Then there was poor, doomed Toulouse-Lautrec. That man drank too much absinthe and felt most at home in a house of prostitution—to paint a naked lady.

What propels this conversation, I think, is that we're both trying to figure out if we are artists—an agenda we rarely acknowledge but which selfishly drives our research. At this point we have established, after thorough review, that the truest artists run hot, are lascivious, are mentally or physically sick, and/or had near-death experiences as children.

The Old Blind Man once explained to me that his mother took him at age six to a special art school in New Orleans to get tested. When they stood him at an easel, he painted a burning house, and they said, Yes, the little boy's an artist.

Soon after the test, however, he broke his wrist wrestling with the neighbor boy. An inexperienced medical resident then overdosed him on ether. And when his mother brought him back to the art school, they apologized and told her, No, I'm afraid he's not an artist.

Family of Saltimbanques

Describing her first performance at the St. Mark's Poetry Project, during which she wore black snakeskin boots and sang her poems to music, magnetic poet–punk rocker Patti Smith claims, "It came, I felt, too easy . . . I decided to back off."

In art, I fight for unconscious creation. Labor destroys painting. (German Expressionist Emil Nolde)

I have always tried to hide my own efforts and wished my works to have the lightness and joyousness of springtime. (Matisse)

My professor has us read Browning's *My Last Duchess* aloud and asks if we can hear how beautifully Browning disguises the craft—everything is so enjambed that you don't hear the couplets. This, explains the professor, is "bravura flourish": to write in a form and disguise it.

Picasso was a shape-shifter and used many alter egos in his work: the harlequin, bull, Minotaur, and monkey. Such multiplicity seems appropriate for a virtuoso. (One definition of creativity: associative ease.) I don't think his temporary obsession with *les saltimbanques*, or acrobats, was coincidental either. On some level Picasso must have related to their task: performing gymnastic stunts—leaps and somersaults—with grace and poise. He especially liked to portray them in casual moments, off-stage, their bodies relaxed, almost slumpy, their superpowers concealed.

Last night, during the final minutes of a playoff game against Houston, while watching Kevin Durant sink three consecutive free throws, I became fascinated with the scant bald spots on his closely sheared head—Durant's only visible chinks.

"Sometimes I feel as if I'd like to tie one arm behind my back," Picasso once said, "to make things more difficult."

Young Acrobat on a Ball

The Artist drives with no hands, just shimmying the steering wheel between both knees. He handles a car like a poem, with confidence, in a loose way.

Each of us has to find something that "does it" for us, that makes us come "undone," says the Artist. I envy how clear the whole thing is for him.

I ask the Artist whether writing is ejaculatory. The key is you don't write about lovemaking per se, he says, quoting William Gass: you make love to the *language*.

We've been arguing about efficiency. The Artist prizes it in all activities, including art, whereas I'm inclined to hesitate, to linger.

I want to die of something awesome, the Artist says, like getting eaten by a pack of wolves.

I like a line of poetry ornamented as a bride. The Artist likes a minimal line, a bone gnawed clean by one of Baudelaire's dogs.

Language is everywhere around us, says the Artist—fear of the blank page is neurotic.

The Artist's new book is full of bold propositions—a hundred attempts to be loved and a hundred attempts to be hated. I have no such caprice in my bones.

When I tell the Artist that I'm looking for a voice, he says that's preposterous because you *begin* with a voice. He scoffs. It's all voice, and at the end you just go back and unify it.

The Artist says he had a dream that I was giving a poetry reading and recited a long, lovely poem, but later I turned into an old jalopy, and then my poem went, "Dream. Crash, crash, cachunk, cachunk. Dream, cachunk, cachunk."

I am not writing at all how I like. I never seem to be writing how I like. Whereas the Artist likes to crow from his writing throne on the couch, near the window that looks onto the street and the people and the pothole and the crows and the garbage trucks and the blooming dogwood, on his throne surrounded by dictionary and sourcebooks and coffee, and wearing for warmth a sleeping bag like a royal cape, he likes to crow, I'm writing exactly how I want to write!

At the Lapin Agile

In antiquity there were nine official muses, through whom it was believed inspiration flowed.

Sappho was called the tenth muse because it was the custom of poets, including Dante, Hesiod, etc., to invoke the muses at the beginning of a poem or song. Because Sappho did not consult the muses, and because this would have equaled disaster for a mortal poet, it was said that she must have been part goddess.

Homer's introduction to the *Odyssey*: "Tell me, O Muse, of that ingenious hero . . ." Hesiod's plea in *Works and Days*: "Sing goddess . . ."

Sappho, on the other hand, wrote in a brazen first person that circumvented the conventions of inspiration: "It's no use // Mother dear, I / can't finish my weaving" or "Good grief, gods do what they like."

Parade

While at work on *Parade*, Picasso met Olga Khokhlova, the dark-haired Russian ballerina who would become his wife and, for a time, his muse. During their engagement he liked to waltz Olga around the neighborhood, take her to fancy balls, show her off.

He painted her holding a Spanish fan, seated in a chair upholstered with rich fabric covered in enormous flowers and grapes.

A few years into their marriage, he became intoxicated with a new woman—a young, voluptuous Swedish blonde, Marie-Thérèse Walter. During that time his wife still appeared in his work but as a monster with perfect white breasts attacking him with a stiletto.

Otherwise, Picasso painted fanciful daydreams coded with desire for Marie-Thérèse, imagining her as a peach, a guitar, boomerangs, a gas pump, a bather playing by the seashore, while disguising himself as a jug, a beach ball, a penis running through the sand.

Blah, blah, blah, we've all heard these stories about Picasso before. He liked women, and one of the primary engines of his inspiration was lust, and his style changed with each sensory-stimulating affair. In Françoise Gilot's words, "First the plinth, then the doormat." In Picasso's words,

"There's nothing so similar to one poodle dog as another poodle dog, and that goes for women, too."

Occasionally, Picasso's hand had become accustomed to drawing one lover such that when sketching a new muse, he ended up with a transitional image—a distortion of two faces. This happened in an organic way and was not of much concern.

Reclining Female Nude under a Pine Tree

Inspired by the many spider lily balls floating through the air at Limahuli Gardens in Kauai, the Artist constructs his own creation myth in which children, like plants, are produced by a spreading wind. In his world lovers could just come together briefly and then part. He imagines cottonseeds released from his penis and spreading. But would a woman still have to go through childbirth? I ask, because then she will know the cottonseed baby is hers, and she'll have to take care of it.

The Lovers

"Women are machines for suffering," Picasso once said. You can map his work onto his lovers like an alphabet that ends in "Lady Z," a portrait of his final *amoureuse*.

After countless relationships, the Artist says his philosophy is that people come into our lives and then without any explanation, they go. I hate how Picassian that sounds.

When he tells me, I'll always love you, it sounds preemptive. I'll love you even after you're gone; even after "us" is what I hear.

Writing a book, says my professor, is a life experience, like falling in love is.

When they got married, Melville's wife wanted to farm and he wanted to write, says the Old Blind Man: he wasn't happy with her so he sublimated his feelings and sex into writing. If Melville hadn't married that woman, he never would have written *Moby-Dick*!

When I asked the tarot reader about my heart, I drew the devil card. A man and a woman posed naked at the center of the card, a triangle covering the crotch area. They were sharing a body, coming from one root.

The reasons she broke up with me were the things I like the most about myself. So things probably weren't going to change. She couldn't handle the substance of my dream, for example. And my petulance—she didn't like my boyishness. (overheard)

If we're still together in six months, we should go to Portland. No, Australia. Are we together? I ask.
Yes, says the Artist.

On a walk yesterday, I noticed that some photos of a man and woman had been thrown into the bushes on Roy Hill. I wonder which of them did it.

My neighbor says she's most angry she gave this guy "the last years" of her beauty; that is, her early thirties. She claims she's since lost her metabolism.

Cézanne liked models who were solid, stocky. In fact, he married one of them—a bookbinder named Marie-Hortense Fiquet. Because of the way he painted her—stiff, with an apple-like head—Cézanne's friends nicknamed her "Hortense la Boule" (the ball).

Cyril Connolly says that love is a "grafting" process, and when it breaks up, it takes with it ingrown fibers, ripped right from the root. Reading that description, I can imagine our love ripped right from the skin of my forearm.

You can't have the thing that you are, says the Artist.

Two lovers are walking together by the side of the sea. They are muffled up in coats. She has a red handkerchief on her head. They walk, very proud and careless, hugging each other and braving the wind. (Katherine Mansfield's *Journal*)

Love is like drowning in an inch of water, say the girls lounging around in cafés.

Artificial red roses in a wine bottle with red foil at the neck.

It has always felt discordant being with the Artist, like the jazz music he loves, late works of Coltrane.

The Absinthe Drinker

Young Jackson Pollock was a reclusive drunk who revered Eastern philosophy and jazz and painted alone in his apartment.

He painted *Birth* (1941) around the time Lee Krasner met him—a terrifying vision of life entering the world, represented by something like diseased, red-eyed salmon churning in large spirals.

Hard to imagine falling in love with such a gruesome image as *Birth*, but Krasner did.

Pollock had given up still life and models and, after extensive psychotherapy, had begun to paint instead from an inner, psychological language rich with symbols and heavily emotional.

"Something blew," said Krasner of seeing Pollock's work for the first time, "something was broken, and I felt as if the floor were sinking."

Contending with Pollock's ideas, which she found revolutionary, Krasner abandoned academic painting and produced a series of horrible gray slabs, "three solid years of buildup of gray mass on the canvas," she said.

It was a "violent transition and upheaval," a "black-out," a "gray-out," a "swing of the pendulum," a "dead period," during which everything went "from a loud sound to a grain of sand."

During this dead period, the couple married and moved from New York to bucolic Springs, Long Island. Isolated in the country, Pollock felt empowered to manage his alcoholism. He set up a studio in the detached barn and began making the splashy work that would soon bring him international fame.

Meanwhile, Krasner sensed she was living not with a man but a god, and determined to support his career. She cooked, canned, jammed, and house-cleaned, and painted in a cramped bedroom upstairs, building up each canvas, reassessing, scraping the paint away, and building the canvas up again.

"And you faced a black canvas . . . ," said Krasner of that period. Not a *blank* canvas, mind you.

Woman in a Gray Armchair

My dad calls and he's like, What are you doing? and I'm like, Oh, being critical.

In Krasner's Gray Period, I see myself, my own trials. No sooner have I formed a thought on the page than I question it, watch myself remove it, rewrite the thought, remove the second version, try a third version, remove the third version. Scraping the paint away. What a colossal mess.

It took Jean Rhys twenty years to finish *Wide Sargasso Sea*: "About my book. It is done in the way that patchwork would be done if you had all the colors and all the pieces cut but not yet arranged to make a quilt. No—it is not that I can't bear to let it go—tho' one often feels like that . . . But I do hesitate about *how* to do it."

I took a walk looking for the East River but instead ran into the United Nations building, with its millions of colorful flags outside flipping in the sun, one using the same palette as the next but reversed, or horizontal instead of vertical. The world seemed to have run out of colors, patterns—to see these flags.

My book feels like a tacky old grandma quilt.

In a dream I send my former professor a draft of what I've been working on. Then, without permission, he sends it to another writer, asking, Is there any integration here?

Working hard but with nothing to show for it, much less than the weeds out back.

My book has become an old clothes basket.

Throwing a tantrum, I delete several pages of material. The rejected material sits on the side in a mound, like all the paint (how many pounds?) Krasner scraped away for three years, and must have had to drag down some rickety wooden staircase and dump in the trash out back.

Head of a Hurdy-Gurdy

My mother mentioned recently that her father had a "tortuous colon," not *torturous* in the sense of pain but in the sense of extra twists.

Tortuous comes from the Latin *torquere*, meaning to twist, wring, distort.

Forget the sinus infection theory. After hearing this I have a hunch that my creative problems originate in the intestines—that is, my difficulty filtering and passing matter—and that perhaps I have inherited my grandfather's problematic colon. Maybe this longer colon with more loops is the cause of my slow, nervous approach to making art.

This little cat never ran straight. (Katherine Mansfield)

My professor doesn't have much patience for these theories. He wants to hear the torque in my *prose*, that self-flagellating smack.

Artist, create, do not talk. (Goethe)

My grandmother died of stomach cancer, says the Old Blind Man, and we found out her stomach was just full of unpublished crap. And it was very painful.

Motility of the gut, my mom says, is probably genetic.

Being a writer has a real sexless quality for me. There is a process of deper-sonalization that feels antisexy, anticorporeal.

My cousin gives me a can of dietary fiber to experiment with as a birth-day present—the idea being that more fiber could improve my poetry. Embarrassed by the gift, I leave it under a friend's bed.

The Blue Acrobat

Sometimes, terribly desperate to get published, the Old Blind Man asks if we can march into the university press and demand a meeting with the editors.

We are denied.

I send a letter of inquiry on his behalf to a local literary agency.

We hear nothing.

Per his instruction I ship a manuscript off to Knopf, accompanied by a letter that he has dictated. A form rejection arrives in the mail, along with the untouched, unrumpled manuscript.

Ironically, when we spend our sessions this way (drafting letters, sending off submissions, etc.), the Old Blind Man seems satisfied that he has accomplished a day's work, though I suspect no good news will come. In a perverse way, I enjoy my role in this ill-fated mission, the illusion of being useful. Instead of scraping away, we just seem to paint and paint and paint.

The two of us usually conduct our official business at the café down the street or stake out a table at the neighborhood Greek restaurant, where the Old Blind Man orders pita bread and green tea. He barks dictations and I take feverish notes. The Greek waitress remembers him from decades ago when he used to dine there alone, back when he could see, and would occasionally order a steak. Refilling his tea cup, she rubs his back and speaks to him in a sing-songy tone. As a treat she brings a little dish of *galactaboureko*.

The first time I paid the tab at the register, the waitress asked how he went blind. Glaucoma, I told her. She said she knew that word because it's Greek—it means "can't be seen." I nodded. Then she said I was doing God's work and crossed herself.

Luckily, the Old Blind Man was out of ear shot. On Sundays he always curses the "church people" who clog up the café after services let out, and he has no use for God, or cures, or salves, or healing, or pity. I once read him Raymond Carver's "Cathedral," a famous short story about a blind man, and he wondered why. I thought he might appreciate the intelligent blind Svengali, but he didn't see himself in the character at all.

When we aren't writing proposals, I usually read aloud to the Old Blind Man. For example, he likes to hear a travel memoir from the 1920s written by British nun-sisters who made an evangelical mission to the Gobi Desert. They adventured through China and Mongolia via donkey.

I don't know if they ever converted anyone, or whether they got lost, etc., because after the first few chapters the Old Blind Man always gets bored.

The only book we have ever managed to finish is the journal of Katherine Mansfield, the New Zealand short story writer who came down with consumption and died at thirty-four.

I'm guessing the Old Blind Man took a morbid interest in getting to the end of the book—the death of an artist fascinates him.

I secretly fetishized this journal, too, because of Mansfield's lack of self-confidence, in part brought on by her disease: "My Eternal Question . . . What is it that makes the moment of delivery so difficult for me?"

Mansfield spends a lot of time looking out the window, at the sky or sea, celebrating nature, and equal time chastising herself for failing to write like Chekhov. In the introduction to a short story collection, editor Marjorie Kinnan Rawlings describes Mansfield as a master raconteur, yet time and again the journals reveal the writer's bottomless self-doubt (one might argue that the short story, in and of itself, is a form that capitulates).

On November 15, 1914, she compares herself to her husband, the writer and editor John Middleton Murry: "The book to be written is still unwritten. I can't sit down and fire away like J."

Mansfield and her husband disagree about how to approach her tuberculosis. Murry beseeches her to seek the best modern-day medical treatment available, meanwhile Mansfield flees to a spiritual community for the promise of a progressive, nonmedical intervention. After just three months of trying to purify her body and soul, which lasts only a page or two in the journal, K. M. dies of a massive tubercular hemorrhage in Fontainebleau, France.

When I visit next, I suggest that we read Mansfield's famous story "The Garden Party": I know I have to shift gears right away, because the Old Blind Man will perceive any lull in our productivity as dangerous. He is sitting in his kitchen on a stool, trying to finish two small pieces of cantaloupe but distracted, telling me we have to publish Katherine Mansfield's journals immediately. He's so excited that he's almost shaking—looks about as deranged as Picasso's *Madman*. But they've *already* been published several times, I explain, semiexasperated (this is an old power struggle of ours). I list for the Old Blind Man all the reasons why I don't think reprinting Katherine Mansfield's journals will make us rich (he has convinced himself that we're going to be rich).

Well, he finally says, quiet and sort of slumped over now, then what in the hell have we been doing all these months?

The great ballet choreographer George Balanchine wanted his dancers to understand that their bodies were instruments. Wasted motion and wasted energy wasted the instrument, and extra rehearsals taxed the instrument, too. The body stretches like a piece of elastic, and over time loses its shape.

Paradoxically, Balanchine taught his dancers to move very, very fast as a way of extending the range and life of their instruments. If you only move a little fast and a little slow, explains one of his former prima ballerinas, you've narrowed your musical range and your *life*.

At nine months pregnant, a friend asks me to accompany her to an appointment to listen to her child's heartbeat through a monitor. The nurse says it's simple: we're listening for movement of the baby, "acceleration."

Charles-François Daubigny tried to paint the fleeting quality of Nature by using "unrefined, rapid brushstrokes."

Notre nature est dans le mouvement; le repos entire est la mort. (Pascal)

Balanchine's dancers were long-limbed and quick, often compared to greyhounds.

When I bemoan how slowly I work compared to the Artist, a friend says, Well, he's in his body, he's "a vital." She means a physical person who needs to move energy around.

Before the discovery of the human egg, the ancient philosopher Galen asserted that women had semen but that the female seed was inferior. The problem was that female semen had much less pneuma (the principle of motion) than male seed. "The female semen is exceedingly weak," wrote Galen, "and unable to advance to the state of motion in which it could impress an artistic form upon the fetus."

Examining the surface texture of Lee Krasner's *Igor*, a portrait of the man she dated before Pollock, scholars find a combo of thick, spontaneous marks along with many reassessments, recalibrations, and revisions: "Grace was received at a cost," wrote one art historian.

It took me about three hours to write [the story] finally. But I had been thinking over the décor and so on for weeks—nay, months, I believe. (Katherine Mansfield re: "Taking the Veil")

Load, aim, fire. (Philip Roth)

Galen asserted that without a man, a woman's semen was so weak that she could not even generate "moles" or misshapen lumps (most likely, the hard lumps he meant were uterine tumors, cysts, and large hydatidiform moles, which he thought grew only after a woman had intercourse with a man). Theodotus the Valentian supported Galen, claiming that what the female seed produced alone would be "weak, formless, and imperfect."

Theodotus and Galen must have known that in Greek mythology the world began in "chaos," though chaos didn't mean what it now means. Chaos was an inert lump: a clump of porridge, a tumor. This lump preceded form. It was a conflict.

The Artist and I get into a fight after going to the art museum downtown, where we watched a limber dancer—almost a contortionist, really— perform in front of a mediocre sixteenth-century Italian painting depicting the moment Atalanta loses a footrace to Hippomenes and his golden apples. The dancer has set up a series of obstacle courses in front of the painting she must navigate around—wine glasses and ceramic lemons. At the Q&A following the harrowing performance, the dancer explains that her personal mantra is "failure is an option" and that she even has a hat printed with the slogan. Later over martinis the Artist says he admires that the mantra articulates in a clever way that failure is never inevitable—that when it happens, it was always a choice. I disagree, saying I find the slogan beautiful as a celebration of failure, an admission that failure is crucial to the process of making art. The Artist repeats himself. I rephrase myself. We go around and around until at a certain point it becomes clear that the subtext of our argument is my book and whether I will ever finish it.

Well, you can have any mantra you like, says the Artist in a huff, as long as you actually do the work, as long as you *make art*.

Portrait of the Artist's Mother

You'd think it would be no big deal, a dinner of leftover Indian food, says my dad, but your mother spends four hours heating up a bunch of dishes and then cleaning up the kitchen. She spends so much time undoing what she's done, he says, and then putting back together what she has unraveled.

My mother has a prodigious vocab, informed by Latin, Italian, and French, and what can only be described as a rhizomatic memory. She can track data over seemingly infinite space and time. Every attempt on my part to tighten a sentence, to remove the dross, to drive the argument forward, to forge a linear narrative, represents a rebellion against my mother's loquaciousness—the person who must have taught me speech patterns.

Another theory yet. I wonder to what extent the people who raise us also raise our words, our language, our syntax. My mother was entertaining, says the Old Blind Man, and my father carved the turkey. "Would you like my stuffing better if it was more oniony? I thought it was kind of lackluster" (my mom).

She tells some anecdote and I say, What's the nugget? What are you getting at? Even though that's exactly what I myself don't do either. She speaks in apparent tangents that eventually wrap back around, if you have the patience to sit there and let them play out.

Pregnant Woman

Once at MOMA in New York, eating a latticed spinach croissant out of a wax paper bag, I studied Picasso's *She-Goat* in the courtyard below, visible through the tall glass picture windows. Snow fell on her head and back and piled in the hollow, cylindrical pit of her belly.

My sister, a third-year medical student, recently told me about "the movements," the adjustments a fetus makes on its way through the birth canal.

This reminded me of yoga class, how we learned about the torque of the kundalini spine, three and a half times twisted around itself, along which the yogi's energy travels.

Does a poem or essay or book behave as such? Expressing a certain set of movements on the way to completion? Wrapping itself three and a half times around a question?

After all these years, poor *She-Goat* is still expecting.

Self-Portrait at Thirty-Six

Sometimes I find myself thinking about how Gertrude Stein's *Tender Buttons* has no narrative yet is the underbodice of a story.

Stein seems to imply that while our lives parade as dramas, as theater, on the underside they're composed of a long sequence of painfully simple events; for example, the hundreds (it feels like thousands) of times I've ovulated since age fourteen—all that production.

I bet my body looks at me and thinks, What an idiot.

These days I'm beginning to face my failed role in these performances, though my body, at least, did not fail to mold its little masterpieces. "In white in white handkerchiefs with little dots in a white belt . . ." (from Gertrude Stein's "Egg" poem).

The smaller it is, says my mother, the more expensive.

Dwarf Dancer

Beginning in 1946 Lee Krasner gave up her easel. When she did that, something new began to "come through" (this is her language, and in it you can hear the influence of Pollock's psychotherapeutic lens).

"I believe in listening to the cycles . . . If I am in a dead working period, I wait, though those periods are hard to deal with," she said.

Krasner began working at a desk or on the floor, applying paint straight from cans with sticks and palette knives. During this period she produced twenty-seven known canvases, which she called the Little Images, none more than three feet tall.

One art historian said the work resembled a dropped can of pick-up sticks and noticed in it an agitation not present in her earlier work. These paintings had "a new energy" in which Krasner "first established a tension between chaotic, all-over patterning and systematic structure."

Shellflower, 1947, explodes with jazzy triangles in loud colors.

In *Composition*, 1949, the whole canvas seems encoded with geometries, triangles, balls, and bricks, scrawled in an unreadable Hebrew.

Untitled, 1949, plays with an alphabet of gray shapes that resemble bones—gray scarabs, small ladder-shaped spines, old skulls, old teeth, and hints of color. Look twice and you'll realize this picture is a sort of gray slab with shapes and colors that have danced up through the muck: "I felt fantastic that something was beginning to happen after all this time where there was nothing, nothing, nothing."

According to one historian, the frustration and lack of productivity Krasner experienced during the Gray Period recurred for the rest of her life. Though she tried to view dead periods as natural, they were painful and humiliating.

As for Krasner's Little Images, the reception then and now is mixed. Some viewers applaud the energy of this series, constipated as it is, and delight in her uberclumpy impasto, while others dismiss these paintings as overworked.

(No doubt the ancient philosopher Galen reincarnated as an art critic would've panned them.)

But more than anything, it's the stature of the Little Images that fascinates me, the fact that an artistic breakthrough three years in the making took place on such a small scale.

What's the opposite of gigantism?

Maya with Doll

From about 1935 to 1949, sculptor Alberto Giacometti experimented with scale. In his imagination he saw large figures, but his hands translated these figures inaccurately and most of the works during this period came out no taller than three inches: "I need to make it very small so that I have control over the figure," he wrote to dealer Pierre Matisse.

During this somewhat traumatic decade, when World War II hit and the artist's mother died, scholar Casimiro Di Crescenzo writes that "Giacometti found himself reducing the size of his work further and further and further until his sculptures vanished, as he later confessed, 'into dust.'"

This process resulted in what looks like a collection of little worry dolls cast in bronze.

In my heart I deeply relate to Giacometti's experiment. This book is a miniaturization of my ambitions, is simply a record of a few passages that did not vanish over the last ten years of my life, which also happens to have been my reproductive prime.

Portrait of Maya

The Artist's only child is the kind of kid who builds fairy houses out of moss and sticks. She likes to walk in the mud barefoot and decorate her foot-molds with leaves and grasses. I sense that most of the time she's wrapped in a sort of magical cocoon of childhood.

She can spend three hours lost in her dollhouse, playing with chestnuts that she has collected and dressed in little rags, rearranging the furniture, and whispering to herself.

She squirrels away scraps of fabric, pinecones, string, champagne corks, carpet samples, and paint chips, even fuzz—anything that might transform into a dollhouse accessory.

During bath time I often sit next to her on the toilet seat. She tells me about feuds at school that day, and her best friend's crush. She swirls plastic animals through the water, always half-distracted by the stories she creates with her toys. At the end of bathtub talk, the tub is usually full of grass.

By her bed the girl keeps a "body cup," she tells me. When I ask her what that is, without any self-consciousness she says, That's where I put everything that comes out of me at night—mostly hair, boogers, fingernails, and spit.

The Factory

Hilma af Klint's painting *Childhood #1* depicts eggs that hold twin flowers, and the flowers—much like eggs—hold smaller flowers.

On some level this is an image of production, of the factory of life almost. Which came first? The egg or the flower?

Female babies are born with all their eggs, which then release over the course of decades, until menopause, so that from the start baby girls are flowers packed with caviar.

You have to be careful when you marry a beautiful woman, says the Old Blind Man—some of them age well, but others go to seed.

After twenty-some years, I finally get that the menstrual cycle is a technology, like the internet, dry cleaning, or Art.

Maternité

Come March a few green leaves sprout through the dead carcass of morning glory on the wall, its twisted mass black with rain.

Then, as if the world feared its own emptiness, as if the world—like Adam and Eve—realized it was naked, life springs up everywhere.

Yesterday, over the garage roof, one magnolia blossom had opened. Today there are seventeen more.

"Let the earth sprout vegetation," says the God of Genesis.

Come spring, morning glory buries the stray cinder block.

In the sun the black pug pants like a snake.

The cherry tree wields its shish kebab of flowers at the sky.

"Fruit trees of every kind on earth that bear fruit with the seed in it."

The thirteen-year-old wears a high ponytail but leaves two long strands in front to frame her face. I haven't seen this look since *I* was in seventh grade. What do the strands signal? Are they like presexual fringe? Like leashes for pulling. *Temptation* comes from the Latin meaning "a testing."

New face—same ol', same ol'.

Flowers are followers.

No tree is remiss to bloom.

After the breakup of a long relationship, she cuts her hair, the bangs dangerously short. The pixie is a look she had years ago—she has the cheekbones for it. Life is just a carousel of hairstyles.

He shaves his neck, leaves the beard, and trims the whiskers that tickle his lips.

New life surges into the landscape as we decay.

Spring is mechanical.

They were always competitive about careers, boys, and beauty—now it's husbands, houses, and babies.

"The fruit tree (whose seed is in itself) making fruit after its kind, on the earth."

Birth of a child: for us, the closest thing to spring.

The organicism of [Krasner's] process has been located, both by herself and by scholars, in its cyclical character . . . impulse or seed and a flowering of intensity, followed by a period of dormancy, quiet, without work. (historian Katy Siegel)

A friend confides her "neck is starting to go." In the last year, multiple men have bought her drinks and then demanded her age. When she resists, they try to guess instead: You're about twenty-six. No, wait a minute, they say, pointing to her crow's feet, you could be midthirties actually . . . or even early forties.

I'm trying to remember to put jojoba oil on my face every night, a face that feels like an old mitt.

Asked about the classics, Jamaican writer Marlon James says he adores *Pride and Prejudice*, and even though she is shrill and sexist, his favorite character is the mother, Mrs. Bennett, because she's the only character that recognizes that her daughters will not be marriageable for long—she's the only one who feels the mortal crisis, who "knows what time it is."

White cherry blossoms, sad white sky.

The flower in bloom is but half-unfolded.

Spring means varicose veins again.

This spring I feel like the fading flower, the nibbled-up leaf (not the tree that will bloom again).

Finished tulips like broken umbrellas. In this weather all the skinny girls are ready to strip, be sad, sexy, and warm.

For our thirty-seventh birthdays, we go for pho and discuss our fertility: My late spring no bud or blossom shew'th. (Milton, sonnet 7)

This morning seagulls cry, painting spring with their cliché melancholy.

Spring hides behind its gauche colors.

By May 1 the leaves are a leathery fact.

An old lady wearing all red, her scraggly white hair tucked under a red hat, a pair of bug-shaped sunglasses hugging her face, hobbles down Polk Street toward Fern in red stiletto boots. Two old-lady humps stick up through her dress, interrupting the silhouette. The woman's tiny, chicken-legged body hides inside this costume such that she is all accoutrements.

The young wear their beauty, the old their jewels and lipstick.

[Colette] opened a chain of beauty salons from which her clients emerged looking fifteen years older. (from Edmund White's little book on Paris)

The elderly can be beautiful, too, but only like dried flowers.

"And the earth gave forth . . ."

Spring

Spring felt sadder than ever this year, just keying in to the drama of the plants and trees flowering, fading, and dying back. In March a sunny day tricked the flowers open, then in May the rain removed all the petals and matted them to the driveway like little white condoms. Cyril Connolly: The heart is meant to be broken, and after it is mended, to be broken again.

I kept thinking about that anecdote in the film *Sans Soleil* with the Japanese man whose wife dies one winter yet it's not until spring that he commits suicide. Spring as unbearable. Spring as a sham.

On top of that, my young neighbor in the building next door whose windows line up perfectly with mine was having a decadent romance. Candlelight dinners every night, endless nudity. I could hardly stand the intensity of it, and the way it seemed explicitly tied to the magnolia blossoms.

Nude in Red Stockings

The poet I've been reading lately is such an exhibitionist, writing mostly of her sexual prowess, her infidelities, in hopped-up lyrics, like some cross between Mick Jagger and Gerard Manley Hopkins. On the back flap of the book, a famous poet praises the diversity of her syntax. I have noticed this quality, too, and the way it feels like a slew of new sex positions on every page.

The Beast

Gauguin named his dog Pego, which means "penis." At the time he lived near a Catholic girls' school and would call for the dog so that students and teachers in the schoolyard would hear him calling "penis, penis."

Theory: I sometimes worry that artists are more animal than I am—with raccoonish hands, bat ears, propulsive dog-like digestion, the most sensitive noses and pricks—extremely mortal.

The Artist confesses he has a fear of lightning. He says maybe he feels it too much in his body, like a horse.

The poet tries to shock us with her moaning yeast infection poem, tube top, leather skirt.

Through the Artist I have learned to pay closer attention to the natural world. He has taught me a new form of sensuality.

Flowers that open like vaginas, leaves that sprout like penises.

Picasso said everything has to be natural. And that's how he made art and that's how he carried out relationships.

"Artists have lost all their savagery, all their instincts," wrote Gauguin in his last letter. "Everything I learned from other people stood in my way."

Cocteau once said of Picasso that his eyes were like the coal black butt of a gun. He meant it as a compliment, as if to espouse to Picasso's eyes the quality of prodding phalluses.

The hibiscus flower is grandiose, with a stamen that protrudes stiffly as if to sniff drugs. The flower petals are tribal pink, the color of passion.

La belle hollandaise

The Old Blind Man and I have been reading an article about beauty. The argument is that certain kinds of beauty are universal because they connect back to human evolution, to survival of the species, to our experience back in the savanna—the beauty of a baby's face, or of a central California landscape, for example.

The author says Darwin used the word *beautiful* to describe a peahen's feeling for a peacock's tail (i.e., that which is beautiful may inspire procreation).

As we read, the Old Blind Man is reminded of a painting his older brother— long deceased—had raved about seeing in Amsterdam during World War II: Rembrandt's *The Night Watch*. We look up the painting on my phone. I explain to the Old Blind Man that it's one of those complicated scenes crowded with figures and symbols—for example, a man in an oak leaf helmet, a girl in a yellow dress with the claws of a dead chicken fastened to her belt. It is famous for being enormous, coming in at 12 x 14 feet (of beauty).

My brother didn't tell me that, says the Old Blind Man, wondering if we can call the Rijksmuseum and get a copy of it (when you make a call for the Old Blind Man, he sits on the floor and you hold the receiver to his ear and you always feel like you're phoning from the White House). You want a postcard? I ask. Well, I don't *know*, he says.

Recently, I visited a museum and saw Krasner's *Untitled*, 1949, from her Little Images series. Until that point I had only seen reproductions, and in person it had a congested look. I could tell it was an image that she belabored until the paint—the consistency of toothpaste—became almost architectural. *Untitled* hung on a small wall next to a large work of Pollock's, one that felt spacious and free.

Famously, when asked, Do you work from Nature? Pollock replied, I am Nature.

Aeschylus: There is no effort in what is divine.

The Artist argues that writing poems feels right, whereas editing his work for consumption—making it into a book—feels wrong. A plant or flower doesn't grow in order to become beautiful, he says. It grows because that's what it does. That's natural. We may watch it grow, but it doesn't grow for us.

Art is a fruit that grows in man, like a fruit on a plant or like a child in its mother's womb. (Jean Arp)

Maybe that's the very crux of talent. Maybe more so than a frustrated artist, what the natural artist contributes to society resembles the flower or fruit produced by the tree—the peach, the kumquat, the apple—and that is why we love to consume it.

Nude in a Garden

It feels like more women are pregnant than ever before. I watch their fruit-shaped bodies slip out from inside parked cars and hobble along the sidewalk in polka-dot shirts or fashionable jumpsuits. They don't so much project beauty as leak it.

At a party one night, someone claims that pregnant women emit a chemical that makes other women want to be pregnant. "I *believe* that," one of us responds—"I just stare at those bellies. I can't help it; I want to touch them." Melinda says that some pregnant women report waking up in the night on their way out to the garden to eat dirt, while others take capsules of soil, for the minerals. I think to myself, "The body is a farmer" (Lyn Hejinian).

At the neighborhood café, I take note of pregnant ladies with huge purses.

Across the street one sidesteps a greasy pizza box, her ponytail bouncing.

Another tattooed pregnant woman emerges, birds wrapped around her upper arm in a wiry style.

Abalone, clams, oysters, mussels, marine snails: any mollusk that produces a shell can produce a pearl.

Steph sends video of just her belly and feet—she must have propped the camera on her chest, right where her pregnant stomach begins to jut out. The baby swims in place, undulating Steph's skin and the entire globe of her.

Riddle: a red, round house with a star inside.

At a picnic a friend of a friend sits with legs woven through each other, abstaining from beer, her face tan from sun and her skin rubbery from the births of her children. The first one came out Cesarean, she says, because she had not yet discovered the breath-work and opening of the hips that yoga introduced. While we talk I half-study her form (round again with another child), her smoker's voice, her finger tattooed with a wedding ring design that matches her husband's.

One of many Aztec rituals devoted to fertility involved sacrificing a beautiful virgin, says my tour guide at Guachimontones, a set of round pyramids near Guadalajara. She would be skinned and the priest would then perform prayers wearing her skin.

Answer: an apple.

A friend's six-year-old calls a bikini comically a "vikini."

Imagine that you are back in the water, in the sea, in the womb, my yoga teacher likes to say, and that your joints are incredibly supple. Breathe like a fish: let your ribs open and close like Venetian blinds.

The ancient Indian epic known as the *Ramayana* tells the story of Anjana, who badly wanted a child. She went outside and prayed to the gods. She held her hands out to the sky, searching for a sign. The god of wind, Vayu, took a fancy to Anjana and sent grains of rice down into her cupped palms. Soon after she became pregnant, immaculately.

Most of what we call beauty is just fertility on parade.

In a Rauschenberg collage a quarter of a mile long, I'm drawn to a pregnant belly tattooed with a simple butterfly.

Butterfly Hunter

Once, during the time my mom was pregnant with me, she came out of a grocery store in Hyde Park, a neighborhood in Chicago, and a guy pushed her over with all her grocery bags and tried to take her purse. In the moment she struggled with him and triumphed (no one steals that lady's purse from right under her nose) but it was still scary, and my dad ended up gifting her a necklace with a little butterfly charm to wear as a protective talisman. He nicknamed the butterfly Milt.

If this book had a charm, a talisman, a Milt, I wonder if it would have found its way.

As I was trying to finish this book, it struck me that I was thirty-two years and five weeks old, the exact age my mother was when she had me. Two years and two weeks later, I turned the age my mom was when she had my sister, and my mother's productivity overwhelmed mine.

I remember reading that while pregnant with the baby that would become women's rights activist and godmother of vagina-art Judy Chicago, Judy's expectant mother wrapped her large, pregnant belly in a ribbon tied with a bow.

Maybe it is only women in their thirties who begin to equate (conflate?) books and babies, art and babies. Like the culture, we expect ourselves to bear some sort of fruit. In reality babies resemble books much more than the other way around, in that we are all texts that in the beginning, page by fluttery page, our parents read, and that later our lovers read, and that later everyone forgets to read.

Woman with Her Hair in a Bun

Several of the little meditations in Marguerite Duras's *Practicalities* treat the subject of lost, forgotten objects, like the two-hundred-year-old women's underblouse speckled with pink stains that Duras discovered jammed at the back of her antique dresser when one day she removed the middle drawer, or the tortoise-shell hair clips she happened to find underneath a floorboard in her apartment. Duras deals in the secret lives of the material world and the secret dealings of people—lies, cover-ups, the beauty nestled inside shame.

My mom says men don't understand that women need to constantly freshen up their wardrobes to feel good. Next thing I know I'm wasting time on the internet looking at linen jumpsuits, designer clogs, earrings shaped like clusters of grapes. But after an hour or two this seems fruitless. I don't feel vivacious these days, so what's the use in decorating myself in expensive accessories.

Or is it just that I hate my taste—that my taste is so weak, suggestible, self-conscious, that I don't know how I want to adorn myself?

In Elif Batuman's *The Possessed*, the author asks what a person's belongings say about him or her. She suggests that objects form a sort of riddle about us. If I died, it would probably disappoint my loved ones to find mostly notecards, tarnished jewelry, hair-ties that have lost their elasticity, books full of yellow highlighter. That's what they'd have to remember my soul by.

Japanese Divan

At my age, as a woman, you're supposed to have both professional accomplishments and children, or if you don't have children you should at least have accomplishments, or if you don't have accomplishments in other areas, that's explained away by the cherubs at your feet.

Picture, for example, Renoir's portrait of Madame Georges Charpentier, circa 1878, lying back on her trendy Japanese divan, one blond child sitting at her breast, the other blondie in a matching blue romper lounging on the back of the large family dog, a dog whose coloring coordinates with Mrs. Charpentier's long black skirt finished with white lace trim. A rich gold Japanese screen decorated with peacocks sits behind the family, embracing them in golden warmth, and in the background, just beyond the couch, set on a stylish rattan table, a bouquet of flowers, a dish of grapes, and a carafe of sweet wine and serving glasses, ready to enjoy.

Visually, we're invited to correlate fine taste with bounty, aesthetic sophistication with fulfillment, the golden grapes in the bowl on the table with the unidentifiable golden object that Mrs. Charpentier rustles around in her left hand, like the golden coins of Lakshmi—goddess of abundance, wealth, and complete expression.

In one of my apartments, all I had on the walls were Post-it notes on which a friend had suggested what might hang there: Botticelli's *Birth of Venus* or a

Hokusai in the bathroom; a Dutch still life with vases, flowers, and fish in the kitchen; black-and-white street scenes in the living room. Quite a far cry from Madame's highly coordinated haute-Japanese theme, but I preferred these provisional notes in my friend's handwriting to any poster that might have hung in a cheap frame; I preferred the blank walls, their yet-to-be quality.

A few years later, the windows of my next apartment looked down on a corner where a neighborhood free pile often formed. I regularly dragged furniture and objects in from the street, appreciating the random quality of such items—a turquoise vase, a large glass tureen containing brilliant yellow-green fake moss, a wooden chair with red plaid cushions that soon disintegrated.

The reason your apartment has a hodge-podge aesthetic, said the Artist, is that you say yes to everything.

Once, out of curiosity, I spent a night scrolling through a website a friend said she liked that sold rugs and plant baskets and woven plates augmented with colorful tassels and pom-poms. The website showed some gorgeous bohemian woman in Byron Bay, Australia, handcrafting all of these products in not much more than jeans and a black lace bra, a jungle of shiny houseplants cresting in the background.

In one picture her small child lay naked on his back on one of her rugs, which presumably she'd woven on the standing loom in the distance.

When does one learn to act like a normal woman—the kind who keeps houseplants, weaves, uses color swatches, and plans her lingerie?

The Artist's apartment can look cobbled together, full of mismatched furniture, the décor uncoordinated, and I swear there's something charming about it, partly because he's a man.

In theory I can do whatever I want, too. Yet there's an expectation that as a woman I'll *make* a home.

House in a Garden

Yesterday, after scribbling in my notebook all morning what I soon realized was page after page of garbage, I met a friend for coffee and lunch. These days she's focused on downsizing, decluttering, renovation, a redesign of the backyard. She lets slip the name of her first child, due in a few months.

My friend and I used to talk about the mind, the soul, religion, painting— now it's all décor, and what it means to be house-poor.

Interior Scene

Wealthy socialite Mona von Bismarck loved the color white. Together, she and her interior decorator fashioned an all-white drawing room. The white walls and huge bouquets of flowers brought in from greenhouses "echoed her own cool beauty, as well as her view of perfection."

Decorating can take years, but finally the look is set, the vision carried out, and there is not much to do except sit inside and wear it.

The corpse of an individual dated seventy thousand years before the Paleolithic era was buried in a cave in Shanidar, Iraq. Using pollen analysis, scientists determined that the body was laid on a nest of branches and flowers one summer. Even that far back our ancestors were stylists.

When Krasner suffered from creative blocks, she still walked along the beach and collected driftwood, shells, minerals, and rocks, which she then displayed around the house in little groupings. She liked to fill the house with colorful fruits, vegetables, gourds, and dried flowers.

Decorating is autobiography. (Gloria Vanderbilt)

I wonder if good taste correlates to evolutionary fitness, to having the kind of astute ears, eyes, and nose that could outsmart predators, track prey, spot berries in a thicket, single out the most desirable mate.

People care more about being thought to have taste than about being either good, clever, or amiable. (Samuel Johnson)

For a Tulum beach house effect, choose brown leather furniture, neutral linens, baskets, green glass, drapey macramé, and black-and-white photography, says the garish HGTV lady, who earlier in the episode whipped up her own Abstract Expressionist painting to hang over a midcentury modern chesterfield.

At Bar 55 in the Village, the busted ceiling over the bass player's head is décor.

Our taste, says Pascal, comes from our nature. A man's good taste or disgust extends from verse to prose to song to clothes to women.

The Blue Room

What is the *feminine touch*? In Sylvia Plath's "Nick and the Candlestick," Plath speaks to her unborn son in the womb. She suggests that she has hung her womb with the finest rugs for him, "the last of Victoriana," etc.

The womb is yet another place a woman entertains guests—another place a woman decorates, and feeds people.

A Korean friend once told me her mother insisted that a woman's home correlates to her "box." Needless to say, the mother trained my friend to keep a very tidy apartment!

In a subliminal way, a woman's apartment serves as a mock-up for her vagina (sexual apartment) and then, too, for her uterus (reproductive apartment).

Because we work through this world by association, through metaphor, through capsizing two terms into one, a neat, cozy, well-composed boudoir seems to broadcast clean, well-trimmed, well-shaped spaces in the invisible realm. We trust the first image to correspond to the second (the cozy living room leads to the clean, snug pussy, which leads to the soft, safe, happy uterus).

This cascade of associations is how we make decisions, despite all the inconsistencies this method turns up.

Woman with Outstretched Arms

Just because I seem sort of disheveled and can't or don't enjoy taking care of myself doesn't mean I'd be a bad mother—it means I'd be a bad author: I hate talking to, looking at, feeding, primping myself.

In the kitchen, getting some water, I imagine a ghost baby on my hip. That's an image of motherhood I find romantic, never mind the reality of back pain.

I have consumption. There is still a great deal of moisture (and *pain*) in my BAD lung. But I do not care. I do not want anything I could not have. Peace, solitude, time to write my books, beautiful external life to watch and ponder—no more. O, I'd like a child as well—a baby boy; *mais je de mande trop*! (Katherine Mansfield, *Journal*)

At age thirty-eight, a friend informs the doctor she might want a baby. No you don't, says the doctor, you would have figured that out already.

Are you a mother? asks the cashier at the bagel store.

Am I a waste of a woman? a character from Tennessee Williams might wonder in a Mississippi drawl.

You know you can be a complete woman without having children! (Meret Oppenheim to her niece)

And yet, by and large, most of us don't live Oppenheim's wisdom out.

Whether or not I can accept my body as ananthous (bringing no flowers).

Last night after dinner, the Artist's daughter got in my arms. We were all sitting on the floor cushions and she rocked in my arms like a giant baby. Are you nursing? her father teased. She said no but somehow left wet marks on my neck.

Tête de mort

One warm night I went to a ska show at El Corazón, by the highway. A friend's band played the same set they played the time before, with the trumpet player up front in dark sunglasses. We danced. I had recently dropped cardio and my butt felt big.

Next door some skinny, androgynous teenagers were setting up for a metal show. Spray-painted on the side of their van were the words *Skull Fist*. They smoked in the parking lot with their long Axl Rose hair.

I thought to myself, I was never young. I was never, ever young.

Still Life with Steer's Skull

I always assumed that Georgia O'Keeffe blazed forward into art, exploring the desert in her wool gaucho hat, collecting more bones than flowers, and never thought of having children, of her fleeting childbearing years, of her earthly fertility—just her godly powers with watercolor, just mountains and clouds and cow skulls and black hollyhock growing out of the dry orange earth.

The real story is that O'Keeffe wanted a child with Alfred Stieglitz and he refused.

Where I was born and where and how I have lived is unimportant, begins Georgia O'Keeffe's memoir.

This morning there's a blue hole in the clouds, though soon the clouds will break apart, thin, and disappear.

And I think of O'Keeffe's 1943 painting of a cow's pelvis held up to the sky, so that blue pours through the empty center: "A pelvis bone has always been useful to any animal that has it," O'Keeffe once said, "quite as useful as a head."

She kept old pelvis bones all over the house.

She-Goat

Many years before losing his vision, the Old Blind Man received an invitation from a photographer to visit his studio. He had little or no experience with women, and the photographer thought he might enjoy seeing the models nude.

Sometimes the Old Blind Man inquires with the men who work in the fish market or the grocery store about my appearance. At the nail salon, where a Korean woman trims his yellow toenails, he asks her to describe my hair. It's curly, she says. Interesting, he says.

I've been thinking about performing a study of barren women in the Bible, those fallow souls forsaken by God—the body as a desert.

Naked women are the most beautiful thing in the world, says the Old Blind Man. If you're going to have an art lesson, they're going to have you draw basically the female body—not a house or a landscape.

All now regard the barren one as she enters.

Pity her as she collects ovoid rocks on the beach.

Very visceral dream the other day in which my left, inner labia drooped down almost to my knee, hanging and unusable.

A Russian lady in tiger-print leggings calls her niece derisively the "black goat" of the family. I assume she means "sheep," but I like how "goat" sounds more tragic, more homely.

The sky's the color of old milk.

Many times the Old Blind Man has explained that he brought me in because he heard on TV that human contact can keep a person alive. I am so lucky to have *you*, says the Old Blind Man, because somehow you haven't gotten that job or marriage and so you still come and read to me.

In a past life, I probably preferred shawls, robes, capes, cloth that made me disappear.

Sweets

At the café I like to play a game where I imagine strangers moving through phases of the life cycle, each stranger like a sort of riddle. The old melt into younger versions of themselves and the young rapidly age.

Today I notice a twenty-something woman's subtly sexy outfit. She's wearing a white tee, leather jacket that zips at the wrists, blue jeans, a gold watch, black boots, and large silver hoop earrings. The whole point isn't fashion, I think to myself. It isn't what you wear—but whether you're already hot.

I read in a cookbook that when you're baking with chocolate and that delicious, burnt-chocolate smell starts to fill the kitchen and fill everyone in the house with anticipation, that is actually the smell of the chemical complexities of the chocolate leaching away. That is the taste that, now, you will not taste.

Out the café window, an ageless person crosses the street alone, in a drab trench coat, dragging herself across space like a sluggish line painted through a Helen Frankenthaler canvas.

La cuisine

Now that the Old Blind Man has round-the-clock nursing care, many women pass in and out of his house every day.

He holds onto them for balance, taking a measurement of their wrists to guess whether they are thin or fat. He complains to me about the way they make tomato soup or when he detects a strain in their voices.

I've had continual frustration with him this week: his disinterest in what we're reading, his obsession with peeing and moving his bowels. He thinks that to pee is a skill—that some older people die because their penises or anuses don't work. It's been hard to talk about anything remotely interesting to both of us. We walked to and from the restaurant in silence because I couldn't fake joy in conversation.

"You know, Georgia O'Keeffe maintained a very clean diet," I finally offer—"she swore by carrot-celery juice." But lately he is not interested in Georgia O'Keeffe, or anyone.

"I'm much more creative now than I was in the old days," the Old Blind Man responds in the elevator up to his apartment, "because my colon was shriveled up like an acorn—I had to *train* my colon," he emphasizes.

Nude with Drapery

I spent a weekend alone on San Juan Island, snacking on dried apricots and trying to write the book. Instead, I just kept starting at the beginning, looking for a spark of life. Every time I changed the setup, the title of the book had to change. For a while the book was called "Woman with Arms Crossed," then "Girl before a Mirror," then "On Inefficiency."

At one point I called it "Termite Queen," after a strange Meret Oppenheim sculpture made from an exhaust pipe. Oppenheim had a creative block that lasted nearly two decades, during which she left most of her paintings, drawings, and sculptures unfinished and/or destroyed them. Her *Termite Queen* has creepy red eyes.

On the island there was nothing much to do at night, so I went to the community readers' theater in town, where they were putting on a version of Mary Shelley's *Frankenstein*.

A giant gaping cloth hung on stage. A creature—dressed in a loincloth—dramatically emerged from the gaping place in the piece of red fabric, which I came to realize represented a birth scene.

Soon the audience got acquainted with Dr. Frankenstein, his wife-to-be (Elizabeth), and of course Frankenstein's creature—his mad dream—which the doctor had reanimated from dismembered corpses.

The play focuses around the irony that the creature's power to love and ostensibly its desire to mate exceeds the young doctor's. At the most stressful moment of the story, which is about to give way to violence, Elizabeth accosts Dr. Frankenstein: "Oh, Victor, why create life that way when you could just give me children."

Out in the dark theater, I worried that I'd become a sort of Frankenstein too, exhuming bits and pieces from cadaverous notebooks, when I might have—without any intervention or thought or genius—produced a child who could have been a masterpiece. I remembered once a poet-friend gestured at her daughter, in a bouncy-seat on the kitchen counter: "*This* is my opus."

Kids

In the Tantric yoga tradition, desire, or *kama*, is the source of all things. The universe comes into being because it desires to experience itself.

The Artist was a long baby. His mother always says he came out black and blue, like he'd been in a fight.

My sister was born with the umbilical cord wrapped around her neck like a noose, her face blue. The doctor had to pry her out, cracking the clavicle bone, to free the cord.

At the time of his birth, Chagall and his mother were carried on their bed and mattress through the town of Vitebsk, away from a fire, where he was then plunged into a water trough.

"But, first of all, I was born dead," begins Chagall's memoir. "I did not want to live. Imagine a white bubble that does not want to live. As if it had been stuffed with Chagall pictures."

The breath wants to breathe you, says the yogi.

Jackson Pollock came into the world at twelve and a quarter pounds, with—like my sister—the umbilical cord wrapped around his neck and "black as a stove."

Birth is a dance performance, said a mom-friend, for which you can't rehearse.

I have no time to rest. I have only one lifetime in which to force the most exquisite use of the body. (Balanchine)

Ceramist Betty Woodman confesses—perhaps not thinking it would sound shortsighted—that she wanted to have a child simply for the experience of giving birth. I picture Betty pregnant, transformed into a ceramic vessel like the ones she makes. Majolica covered in a landscape of clouds.

When my friend gave birth, she imagined that she was the sand and that her contractions were the sun. As the contractions came on, the sand became searingly hot.

Before he became a writer, the Old Blind Man taught elementary school. But he hated teaching and hated the children. After early retirement in his midfifties, he discovered a passion for riding trains. Traveling on Amtrak, just looking out the window at the passing landscape, the endless horizon, listening to the engine and the train whistle, the Old Blind Man says he felt alive.

During this time he fell in love with the desert landscape and worked with a lawyer and real estate agent to buy up some property in a small town in Utah on the train line. He rode trains frequently until his mideighties, when he began losing his vision.

Recently, the lawyer from Utah called up with an idea that began to obsess the Old Blind Man. The lawyer knew of an Australian land artist who might agree to build a monument on the Old Blind Man's otherwise uninhabited land, a piece of important art, like Robert Smithson's world-famous Spiral Jetty.

For months we corresponded with the Australian and a team of builders who were to carry out the land artist's plans in Utah. The builders sent progress reports and photographs. I would read the reports aloud slowly and describe the photos of cranes lifting pieces of stone in the foreground (in the background the land looked desolate and blank).

The Old Blind Man salivated over these updates and asked to hear them again and again. With each new report from the builders, he felt his life gathering meaning, importance, grandeur.

Finally, the team finished the sculpture. I described the results to the Old Blind Man, the stone tower topped with gold leaf paint to reflect the sun. I assured the Old Blind Man that I could tell from the photographs that the sculpture was imposing, memorable, grand.

For a week, maybe two weeks, the Old Blind Man was ecstatic. The local paper in Utah interviewed him for a story. The local paper in Seattle came by the apartment to interview and photograph him in his favorite red sweater.

He lamented that while most of his favorite writers would be forgotten (hell, Katherine Mansfield was brilliant and had already disappeared), he believed that now he would live on after death. For a small fortune, he had erected not only a monument to the desert but to his own immortality.

He would ask me to describe the sculpture again, the shape and color of the stone, the gold detail at the top, rising toward the sun.

The Old Blind Man has NLP (no light perception) and can only see when he dreams. Often, he still gets anxiety dreams that he's teaching—the classroom returns to him, the little chairs, the monster children. Today, though, the Old Blind Man explodes with joy as he tells me he had a dream about his sculpture: he could see it.

Though the dream was in black and white, like a grainy old movie, he saw that his sculpture was so tall it touched the clouds. He was feeling the sculpture, and it was concrete and it was thrilling! It was more impressive than the Spiral Jetty, he says breathless, grander than the pyramids of Egypt.

I felt like I was high on drugs, says my sister, after she helped deliver a baby for the first time. The attending physician put my sister's hand on top of the midwife's hand to help keep the baby's head from coming out too fast. So it wouldn't rip stuff, she says.

Oh my God, there's a head coming out of there! And it was so squishy, and I thought I was gonna pull off the scalp. I was just standing in shock, says my sister.

A friend hands me her newborn for a few minutes and describes how she gave birth in a portable birthing pool that came in a box, delivered to her apartment as she was going into labor.

She got on all fours in the tub—just a few feet from where we're sitting— hair tied in a high bun, making herself into a sort of sumo wrestler, and reached down to feel the baby's head between her legs.

Out the window I half-watch palm trees swaying against the sky as she talks. Fine fur covers the newborn's little shoulders, like an anorexic woman's.

At first unaware how quickly the skull would mold down into place, my friend says she worried she'd have to teach the child how to live with a cone head.

Woman with Jewels

Socrates's mother was a midwife and his father was a sculptor, and his work as a philosopher arguably fit somewhere between the two. Socrates called his way of looking for the truth *beautics*, meaning the art of giving birth to ideas.

She's having a baby because she's curious to see what it would look like. On a superficial level, she just wants to know what its eyes will be, what its hair will be, what its skin will be.

My mom says she got the jewelry gene, that her great-grandmother sailed to this country with jewels sewn into her coat. Too, her grandmother's name was Pearl (that line of women puts the "Jew" in jewelry).

My dad doesn't care about "stuff," calls antique stores junk shops. He treasures few objects, save for a Harris Tweed jacket he bought as a young man bicycling around Ireland with a poet, before he'd ever met my mom.

The Ayurvedic tradition proposes that we are expressions of our parents' life forces coming together. Within our making is how they felt about each other at that moment, at that latitude and longitude on the planet.

Colette's father was a captain with a wooden leg who spent her mother's fortune from a previous marriage to a madman.

"Eugène Boudin, born in Honfleur on the Normandy coast in northern France, was the son of a mariner," reads wall text at the Frye Museum. "Boudin was a dedicated painter of the sky and sea."

Sylvia Plath, the daughter of a bee scientist, left her stinger in *Ariel*.

Aren't we all but misfirings of our parents, translating them at an angle?

By all accounts Colette was a terrible mother to her daughter, whom she called Bel-Gazou—which had also been Colette's nickname. Once, her daughter tripped and fell, and Colette slapped the little girl and yelled, I'll teach you to ruin what I made.

The new mother posts a selfie to show off the sterling silver nameplate necklace she just commissioned: her infant son's name spelled out in the mother's loopy handwriting.

The mother and baby have exactly the same shade of skin, as if matched by swatch.

According to Edmund White, Bel-Gazou grew up to be a bad student, a spoiled brat, "chronically indecisive," and a huge disappointment to her mother.

Your parents chose each other for their differences, which makes you inherently polar—the parts that don't agree pulling. They probably thought, different as they were, that in coming together they could forge a balanced person.

She has hips and a butt but then a petite (almost scrawny) upper body. He says that walking up the beach in a bathing suit she looks like two different people.

A poet-friend explains that you can only wear jewelry in two places at a time—ears and fingers, or fingers and neck, or neck and wrist, etc. More than two spots, says my friend, overwhelms the eye. My mother never taught me this rule. Then again, I'm not sure my mom understands herself as a composition.

Watermelon Eaters

Dreamed I went to LA, and the Instagram socialite Beatrice Valenzuela invited me to a picnic.

Beforehand, I kept changing my top and ended up in black.

Everyone else wore pastels, including Beatrice's friend, the Insta-stylish Jeana Sohn, and they all photographed each other's hairstyles and the food—frozen watermelon pops and dulce de leche—and of course the children, who cartwheeled around the picnic blanket in designer bohemian bloomers.

Ma jolie

Sally Mann is a mother and artist whose principal subject for many years was her children. Often she would photograph them nude, running around the large, Edenic property in rural Virginia.

"Sally actually had an 8 x 10 camera set up next to the bed—it was a birthing room," says her husband, "and she was able to snap a picture just as Virginia was born."

More so than men, says Judy Chicago, women seek to merge art and life.

I'm very involved in the product—in the final print you put on your wall. 8 x 10 gives that ineffable quality that nothing else does. (Sally Mann)

Jessie, in focus, hip cocked, playing with a long candy cigarette; Virginia at her back, facing the country road behind; Emmett walking the road on stilts, his back to us. Meanwhile, the documentary pans to Mann, who has her head stuck under the hood of an 8 x 10 view camera.

One of Mann's children explains, We lost a mother, but we gained a friend.

Little girl with afro puffs wears pink T-shirt that reads "Mama's BFF Forever."

In the dream my mom warns that when a child is born it legally belongs to the father. She says that when I was five months old she freaked out and had my citizenship changed from father to mother. Did you know that I own you? she says.

As a young man, he began signing his work just "Picasso," his mother's maiden name.

She loves cream, butter, swimming, and her mom.

There are many pictures in which my children are nude or hurt or sick or angry. The children are participants who have been, since infancy, enveloped in my creative process. (SM)

The Old Blind Man was born on January 22, but his mother changed his birthday to March 22, because she preferred a spring baby, an Aries baby, she told him.

To coax her husband into having a third child, my friend prepares a PowerPoint presentation: I delivered it last night, she winks.

He who has made a thousand things and he who has made none, both feel the same desire: to make something. (Antonio Porchia)

Judy Chicago finds that painting bears more connection to the artist's own body than sculpture. A painting comes out of one's body, she explains, while a sculpture is a new, autonomous body.

Mann's son, Emmett, says of himself and his sisters, "We all have that intensity Sally has . . . you can see it in our eyes."

The daughter thinks the mother has too many tchotchkes—little collections and things on the windowsill. The daughter can't see she's the biggest tchotchke of them all.

Girl before a Mirror

It was said of Martha Graham that she was a woman so severe she could have birthed a cube.

The young dancers drawn to Graham enjoyed that she worked them so hard during rehearsals that their bodies ached from fatigue and their stomachs ached from starvation.

Her teaching method required that dancers first master movements on the floor—beginning literally as infants. As they got stronger, they could rise to their knees and then finally to their feet. This training meant to simulate human development.

For performances, as if it were the final and revelatory stage of human evolution, Graham's dancers had their faces painted white and lips red, their upper eyelids blackened, their hair shellacked and parted down the center to form a tribe of radish-head Graham look-alikes.

Self-Portrait

A painter-friend said to me once that artists aren't necessarily nice people. I wonder if that's true, if many artists fail at being warm and generous in the world—if their projects, which seem external, often amount to obsessive self-care.

I read about a hermetic artist who did not even want to own a dog because a dog demands love.

Sculptor Anne Truitt gestures at this perspective when she confesses in her *Day Book*, "It takes a certain stubbornness to keep making objects within the strict discipline of my senses. There is a taproot of selfishness. In narrow fact, I am making them only for my perception."

Plato famously banned dramatic verse from his republic because he worried that artists could damage us by mimicking life on the stage without really caring about the emotional states they mimicked. On very unproductive days, I'm tempted to embrace Plato's skepticism about the artistic project—to see artists as sorcerers and art as an attractive delusion. But maybe that's just a product of my ongoing frustration with writing, my lack of success finding my own way into that blessed circle.

Yo

The old poet now writes strictly in doggerel. The rhymes in his work please him, he says looking up from the podium—do they please us? Well, he says, it doesn't matter. They please him.

Male writers of yore often dedicated books to their wives, as if to say, Sorry again, honey, for my selfish decisions.

Interviewer: Do you write for yourself or others?
Marianne Moore: Myself.

The greatest fault of poetry, says the Old Blind Man, is that no one can understand it.

At the café a real estate agent remarks to the consultant across the table, I need to figure out the problem that I can solve. That's what I want to enable for me.

An artist invents a project and elects himself the president of it.

Parenthood, too, invents its own necessity.

What if instead of asking each other, Do you plan to have kids? we used the language of tax deductions: Do you plan to have dependents?

Irina Nikolayevna Arkadina, the unlikable artist-mother figure in Chekhov's *The Seagull*, spends the duration of the play obsessing over a fading love affair with a famous novelist, swishing her skirts, while neglecting her miserable son.

In almost every photograph, Francesca Woodman caressed herself, or punished herself or dressed herself up. She found transcendence by likening herself to flowers, a stream, lava, moss, wallpaper, but always in the form of a self-portrait.

Pascal got tired of authors referring to their work as "my book, my commentary, my history," since more often than not there was "more of other people's property in it than their own." Would that I could compose a book from the voices surrounding me. Usually I'm more interested in what other people have to say.

Woman with a Large Hat

A glamorous young woman with an entourage of two attractive guys comes up to me in the park and asks if she can paint a picture of my vintage bike, which I happened to borrow for the weekend from a fashionable friend. I lean the borrowed Schwinn against a tree and shyly wait off to the side. She sits cross-legged in the grass, in her straw hat and bare feet and high-waisted shorts. Opening a wooden paint box, she begins, using a compass to sketch the wheels, leaning and rocking her body as she works, almost piercing the canvas with her excited movements. She concentrates so hard that she doesn't say anything when I sneeze. Eventually, she grabs one foot and makes a show of stretching her cramped muscles, then recrosses the leg.

From here I can see that, though she herself looks like a subject straight from Renoir or Toulouse-Lautrec, the image of the bicycle on her canvas is childlike. Yet she doesn't seem sheepish at all.

I'm starting to suspect that art is not thinking but a representation of thinking, that for artists the image remains supreme—appearance above all.

Socrates said, "Become as you wish to appear." It seems to me that most artists go for the reverse, appearing as they wish to become.

The Artist before His Canvas

We wonder why you never see swans floating on a river. I decide it's because—unlike lakes—the river moves rapidly, so they can't see their reflections. Vain creatures.

The poet has difficulty listening to other poets read, unless those poets remind him of himself.

These days, ecopoetics are all the rage.
Egopoetics?
Well, yes. That never goes out of style.

Writing is talking to yourself—it is the talking that no one interrupts.

She travels the world performing her poems. Sometimes I feel like a stand-up comic, she explains, a vaudevillian.

The sky's the color of blue lung.

The Artist admits his superpower is that he's a great mimic. He knows how to steal the music of his favorite writers for his own work, adopting their syntax and their rhythms. Were you always a mimic? I ask. He pauses, swirling a glass of cheap wine. No, he answers, but I always knew how to get away with things. He means that a poet is almost necessarily scrappy, a peddler, a conman, a broker of pawn.

In the dream a successful poet hands me a new "boohoo" poem he wrote (he says that others with that refrain have won awards).

Pascal claims we are (a) self-centered and (b) driven to subjugate others.

For the writers who can only seem to tell a story from first person, who can only see the world from an exposed "I," is that a task of embarrassment? Or grief? Or martyrdom?

During an art walk, I overhear a painter speaking about her work say that she's very proud of the all-red canvas near the back of the little gallery. "Very hot," she says—and I can't imagine talking about my own work this way.

Color is manipulative and willful. The colorist uses it like a puppet to make you fall in love with him.

How vain painting is, exciting admiration by its resemblance to things of which we do not admire the originals! (Pascal)

An artist is an engineer of feelings (Warhol's Factory gets at this directly).

Yesterday in the bathroom I thought, in the parlance of Montaigne, Do I want to be a steward of the world or the word?

She claims she's on a spiritual mission of healing, moving from place to place, channeling vibrations. She writes about war, and global warming, and police brutality, and sex. She deigns to speak for the culture, for the country, for the soul of the world. Her power as a poet and self-ascribed mystic seems inseparable from her personal heat, her sensuality, her big hair, her pretty face, her slammin' bod, her desirability. I'm not blithely traveling around the world, she says.

Poets get sanctimonious and then spend so much time grooming and dressing themselves, trying to look sexy. I guess they do not separate sacred language from seduction.

Marguerite Duras: [Writers] are sex objects *par excellence.*

Self-portrait of the artist after her grandmother's funeral: brooding in a black fur coat and stylish black boots.

The poet is simply a fashion designer, composing new silhouettes, new forms for bodies, clothes for the moon to wear.

He has a soul patch piercing—a small silver stud in the pit above his chin—a fetish, like a shiny seed. Pascal says all elegance is a show of power.

Sometimes the machinations of art—all its devices and strategies to capture an audience—disgust me.

From one view, a cruel view perhaps, I begin to see life as a puppy mill for Art.

Pascal claims "vanity is so firmly anchored in man's heart" that soldiers, cooks, porters, and even philosophers want prestige, and that those who read the philosophers also want it, and that he wants prestige for having written the sentence he is writing, and that I (the writer of *this* sentence) want it for quoting Pascal—in an endless chain like that.

I was thinking about my money, the Old Blind Man says from bed, about buying something special—an important book. What can I buy that's important? What can I do with my life now? That's a really good question, I say.

In 1951 Cecil Beaton did a photo shoot of fashion models posed in front of Jackson Pollocks.

Jackson Pollock: Is he the greatest living painter? (*Life* magazine, 1949)

The poet, I have realized, must use metaphor as a mannequin, styling the poem around this faux body.

Rosamond Bernier hobnobbed with Gertrude Stein and lived around the corner from photographer Dora Maar. Maar had been Picasso's lover and eventually retreated from society, letting her appearance go. Bernier remembers that before Maar started dressing like a bag lady and ignoring the neighbors, she and Maar would sometimes go to the movies together. They once went to see a film featuring Picasso painting on glass. Through the pane of glass, you could watch the famous painter work, brushstroke by brushstroke building up the image. During the film Picasso says, "You can't find truth at the bottom of a well." The line seems to comment on the premise of the film in a clever way. But at that moment Dora Maar groaned to her friend, "Oh my God, if you knew how many times I had to hear that."

I have a friend who perfects a story by telling it over and over, at dinner parties, in cafés, on the phone. I know that what he's really doing is writing. But always to be in control of the conversation, and in control of people's feelings, taking them on a scripted emotional arc—this does a disservice to the uncoordinated quality of life. And in this same way, writing does a disservice to life.

A friend said that I no longer seemed to be writing about writer's block but against writing itself, like the Greeks or Lao Tzu.

You, sitting in that chair all morning, crafting epic poems in tetrameter—you are perverse!

Raymond Carver theorized that art can't change the world, that it's merely entertainment. A higher form of entertainment than bowling, let's say, but still. There had been times when he'd read William Blake or listened to a Bartók concerto or watched a documentary about the construction of an Italian Renaissance cathedral and momentarily thought that it would change him. He was so moved. When the whole thing was over, he would be changed. Then the moment passed, and he was just, well, Raymond Carver.

One must have an ego that is neither too big nor too small, advises the yoga teacher. I spend all night wondering about the size of the ego that is not too small.

Should you be your best on the page rather than in the world—is that fair?

Pascal accused Montaigne of trying to "cut a good figure" on the page, of trying to "paint his own portrait." Did Montaigne anticipate, unlike Pascal, that in the future we would lust collectively after confessions, diaries, navel-gazing memoirs?

A writer must "read promiscuously," William Styron instructs, must take great pleasure in language and have a robust vocabulary, and must have a great theme (though a genius could take a theme that seemed unimportant and make it meaningful). I wonder if Styron includes himself in this Venn diagram, or if he's thinking of *greater* writers than himself.

To publish a book is absurd in such a public culture. What would be the opposite gesture? To bury the book.

After Natalie Portman got the Academy Award for *Black Swan*, a young soloist in the American Ballet Theatre, Sarah Lane, came forward and said that she'd done 95 percent of the dancing. When Lane agreed to let filmmakers graft Portman's face onto her body postproduction, she hadn't realized they would not give her credit. After the grafting it was impossible to tell which scenes were Lane's. I guess it is always the face—not the body—that is dancing.

God is just a pretty thing.

In a dream a spirit comes to my friend and informs her that every book published by someone she knows has the same title: all the books are called *Myself*. Her old professor's book is called *Myself*. Her mother's book is called *Myself*. Her friend John's book is called *Myself*.

Aiming the Deathblow

My professor says there has to be an x factor, that the book I'm trying to write is supposed to "solve for x"—that there has to be something driving the exploration, something burning.

Sometimes he phrases it like this: the writer is supposed to show how he or she "solved the problem of being alive."

I have that phrase written above my desk: "Solve the problem of being alive."

After years of asking me how the book is progressing, my professor shrugs. "You know you don't actually solve for x," he says. "It's a book. You don't have to solve the problem for x in real life—you solve for it in the book. The point is just to write the book."

Woman with Pears

Once, from the bathtub, I compared myself aloud to Cézanne—in temperament. I mean his slow pace, his analytical scowl, his stubborn seeking, and especially the dissatisfaction he felt about his ability to paint what he was trying to paint. I looked at my toes sticking up from the water and sighed, thinking about how hard it was for Cézanne to paint bathers. The nudity of his bathing subjects sometimes excited him too much to finish the painting. Fruit was a better subject for Cézanne, because it did not enlist his emotions, his caginess. Like him, I seem to leave many paintings unfinished.

The Artist was brushing his teeth and listening to my sob story, in which Cézanne and I were both suffering in the same way. But Cézanne *painted*, said the Artist. Your struggle is all in your head, whereas Cézanne struggled at the canvas, struggled with his eye and his brush and his colors.

Woman Washing Her Feet

My dad says, If you treat this book like you're an asymptote approaching a curve, you'll never finish the project. You'll never reach zero. The project could stretch on infinitely, until you die, after you die even, like Antoni Gaudí's cathedral—I don't think that's what you're going for.

Keep moving, says my dad (he probably means so that I don't fall in a pit of despair).

Cézanne recognized himself in the character Frenhofer, the tormented hero of Balzac's story "The Unknown Masterpiece." When old Frenhofer sets out to paint a beautiful young woman, he can manage to paint only one of her feet. No one else perceives the unfinished painting of the foot as a masterpiece, and Frenhofer goes mad.

The Fool

Giacometti's insecurities may have stemmed from problems with impotence, which he blamed on a case of mumps suffered at age eleven, but Giacometti would revive himself by visiting prostitutes, who expected nothing of him. His poetics as an artist, too, was one of failure.

The rain is busy, building nothing.

Outside of biology, we seem to have more use for the word *flaccid* than its opposite, *turgid*.

Krasner just kept walking into the same mistakes, watching herself, probably comparing herself to Pollock, probably sensing the power gathering around his process. She often psyched herself out.

Rae Armantrout: "In order to write / you must fall in love / with your own thought / every time." Not happening.

It's Wednesday and the Old Blind Man and I are having soup and coffee at the Greek restaurant. What are you writing about? asks the Old Blind Man. An Abstract Expressionist artist, I say. Nobody wants to hear about that, he snaps.

My aunt tells me she saw an exhibit of Giacometti's work in France one summer—sculptures, paintings, prints. Even as a teenager, she says, he could sculpt such a realistic head, but he always critiqued his work bitterly. She couldn't figure out what he found so objectionable about these perfect heads of his.

Giacometti: The distance between one side of the nose and the other is like the Sahara, limitless with no fixed points, everything escapes you.

Cézanne stopped working on a painting when he couldn't see how to continue. He often considered his work incomplete and signed only 10 percent of his paintings.

The Artist says I should turn this book into a straight essay on Lee Krasner, more scholarly and academic, that I should drop the first person sections. He says the material about the Old Blind Man doesn't work. Why? I ask. Because he's not that interesting, says the Artist—Do you realize this?

About my book—the trouble is—it is not good . . . I tried too hard. (Jean Rhys)

As you can see, all of these drawings are failures, I greatly regret this but we'll have to start over I hope after the New Year. At this moment, I absolutely cannot draw! (written by Giacometti to his patrons on a portrait of their daughter, *Elizabeth—Head and Shoulders 2*, 1955)

John Cheever once lamented that his writing style had hardly improved over the course of fifteen years. During a move he looked back at his old manuscripts and remarked in a journal entry: I fail to see any signs of maturity, of increased penetration; I fail to see any deepening of my grasp.

Most writers fail without noticing it—like the old, bald poet with no less than three topaz rings on his writing hand, who romanticizes herons and "deaf mutes" in free verse. At least I see my work honestly.

Woman beneath the Lamp

I imagine that when Lee Krasner looked at her paintings, she often saw the flaws. Krasner had a strong Brooklyn accent and the kind of crass, rough, abrupt delivery you might imagine—there was something terrible and sharp about her, which she turned against herself, like the scissors she used to destroy her own drawings beginning in the 1950s, in fits of anger.

"He annihilated those cities and the entire plain, and all the inhabitants of the cities and the vegetation of the ground."

But a few weeks later, when she came back and found her slashed drawings all over the floor, she saw in them the raw materials for a series of chunky collages.

In *Milkweed*, 1955, a collage using oil, paper, and canvas, we find the formal ingredients for a flower: deep black corollas pooling in ponds; piercing white swords up the center of the canvas like stems, decussate against an orange, gray, and yellow background.

For *Bird Talk*, 1955, Krasner cut up her own work alongside Pollock's, incorporating red, olive, orange, and deep pomegranate scraps on an inky black background. Slashes of bright paper suggest bird heads, feathers, tails, leaves, branches.

Winged birds, creeping sea creatures, sea monsters, cattle, animals that creep on land, vegetation, human beings, breath and leaf and thorn and quill and fur and skin. No darkness, no indecision, no doubt, nothing left unwritten—at least for a moment, before the self-critique crept back again.

Without being an art historian, I'd theorize that falling madly in love with Pollock's work posed a huge problem for Krasner. Though she had admired Mondrian and Matisse before Pollock, his ideas struck so deep in Krasner's psyche that for years much of her work ended up looking similar in spirit and arguably derivative of Pollock's. "I believe art is influenced by other art," she once said. Pollock's paintings—not the man himself— were her muse.

After his death Krasner was fond of saying, to describe a particular canvas of her own: "Before Pollock. During Pollock. After Pollock."

Some in the community didn't take her seriously in her own right: "I never went for her paintings. She immolated herself to Pollock. Lee should have had more faith in herself and more independence, but that is the problem with all female artists" (critic Clement Greenberg).

Smoke Clouds at Vallauris

Julian Barnes writes in his collection *Keeping an Eye Open: Essays on Art* that Picasso dramatically simplified art whereas Bonnard dramatically complicated art.

Picasso: I have never made trials or experiments. Whenever I had something to say, I have said it in the manner in which I have felt it ought to be said.

Picasso condemned Bonnard for his uncertainties toward Nature compared with Picasso's own mastery over it, mocking Bonnard for painting the sky blue (as it appeared to the eye) but then adding new colors—a touch of purple, then a touch of pink, etc.

Skeptic does not mean him who doubts, but him who investigates or researches as opposed to him who asserts and thinks that he has found. (Miguel de Unamuno, *Essays and Soliloquies*, 1924)

Algae constantly produce new blades—the stipe grows fastest. You can actually see algae grow, if you're willing to sit there and watch for ten minutes.

The most "successful" people I know would probably reject skepticism as a worldview, as if it were the playground of minds too small to see the problems clearly.

Sometimes you are wrong. Sometimes they are wrong.

Jon Kim Po settles the argument, says the Old Blind Man.

Because Bonnard kept watching the sky, it became a dozen different colors. How hilarious that Bonnard cannot paint a sky blue! thought Picasso.

According to Freeman Dyson, there are two kinds of scientists: unifiers, who leave the world a little simpler than they found it, and diversifiers, who leave the world a little more complicated.

Montaigne used to pace the streets wearing a personal medallion that read "Que sais-je?" (What do I know?)

Pragmatists say truth is what has cash value.

"But facts are a fallacy—an illusion," rants the bearded, emeritus biologist: "The science of Newton has been disproved . . . astrophysicists have come up with new metaphors."

The Artist rubs his nose, encloses his new poem in the rectangle that means done, as he does every morning. For a kiss, he pushes his sharp beard against my blank forehead.

What voice when we hesitate and are silent is moving to meet us? (Susan Howe)

I want more subtlety, less definition—deeper observations, fewer truths.

The Pigeon with Green Peas

The Artist's daughter and I sit on a plaid couch, she's wearing a robe appliqued in cartoon popcorn. I help her draw a giraffe, a cumulus cloud, a squirrel's nest, a spider web.

When she gets bored, we eat wasabi peas and look at a book about hummingbirds. We learn that they have air bubbles in their wings, and that somehow when the light hits these bubbles, it produces an interference that we experience as a jewel-like iridescence.

Caregiving sometimes seems like nothing more than an exercise in helping someone spend their time.

Contemplation

During his first year of school at the Grand Chaumière in Paris, young Giacometti was given a skull from which to make still life. He became so excited to study it that he dropped out of school and spent the entire winter in his bedroom painting the skull.

He longed to define the skull, "to grasp it as far as possible." "I spent days trying to find the root of the tooth . . . which is very high up near the nose, and to trace its course as exactly as I could . . . so that if I had wanted to do the whole skull, it would have been beyond my powers."

At the time Giacometti was struggling to assimilate the parts of a thing with the whole.

In *Dharma Art* Chögyam Trungpa says we should have a "sense of being." We get this through awareness of where we are standing and by opening our sense organs to what is there, such that the edge of a situation slowly dissolves. We begin to notice the way that many tiny things converge, he says, like hundreds of small hairs form an animal's tail.

Cabinet particulier

When evolution comes up with a solution that looks very similar to one that already exists, that is called *homoplasy*, the ichthyologist tells us. For example, the wings of bats, birds, and insects are all "wings." But bat wings include the whole arm and all the fingers, and bat wing skin only stretches in one direction. The hoatzin (or "stinkbird") is a bird with hands. It can climb a tree.

In other words, says the ichthyologist, there is no one kind of wing.

The first definition of *complicate* is to make complex, intricate, involved, or difficult. The third definition is entomological and refers to something folded longitudinally one or more times, as in the wings of insects.

Balanchine tried to strip ballet down. He ditched the ornate music and frilly costumes and did the equivalent to the steps and gestures.

In décor and education and cuisine, we privilege minimalism. We reward those who can reduce. We don't want extra information, no flounce.

Another theory. Love of simplicity: hunting. Love of detail: sewing.

About twenty-five thousand years ago in France, a trend toward miniaturization emerged in toolmaking. Our ancestors increasingly fashioned little borers shaped like stars, scrapers the size of fingernails, and triangular, rectangular, and trapezoidal bladelets, some fitted with saw teeth. One researcher called this phenomenon "an explosion of microliths."

After previous digs microliths were thought to have composed only 2 percent of the toolkits at these western European sites. Follow-up excavations showed that these tiniest of instruments accounted for 72 percent of the total tools used there.

I love how this story illustrates the rewards of looking closer, the complexity available only after archaeologists resifted the same dirt years later through fine mesh screens and water.

My friend who is a hypochondriac says she asked her parents what they thought about her getting a full body scan. Don't do it, said her mother, unless you want them to find something.

Just as the cosmos are infinite, stretching beyond our view in every direction, so is a mite infinitely small, explains Pascal, and so does mathematics have an infinite number of propositions to expound and an infinite number of subtleties and specificities to express.

And even the most sophisticated mathematics, says Pascal, is crude compared to the human heart and mind.

Agnes Martin isolated herself in the desert, where she drew and painted fastidious grids. Often she starved herself in the process. From the outside her subject matter looked monotonous, but she insisted that every point in a grid had its own character. Martin relished the subtlest wiggle in a hand-drawn line. "We are ineffectual," she wrote.

Hummingbird comes, little bolt of hunger, little chest of hubris, whole body wavering.

"If I were not ill," writes Katherine Mansfield in her journal, "I still would have withdrawn from the world because of my hatred of insincerity."

No one can take a picture of the whole sky, the way it looks to me. All portrayals reduce.

The simplest teachings are the best teachings, says a yoga instructor, with conviction, in her Lycra, hummingbird leggings. I'm afraid I seem to be writing against this.

Bird with Worm

At the park, sitting on a bench with my notebook, I try to describe the elegant bum posed on the ledge like a painter's model, the teens eating burgers out of wet, droopy bags, the cell phone towers blinking in the distance.

My professor has accused me of "microscopy." He means I look at small things without linking them to larger literary gestures. He warns that eventually I will have to "map" this book, give it "plot-points," a "gloom," and a "final uptick."

But what of a project like *In the Land of Pain*, the diary Alphonse Daudet kept while dying of syphilis. In the foreword Julian Barnes explains that the book has an "inevitable plot progression" (i.e., the demise of Monsieur Daudet) while still "remaining a collection of notes."

In Daudet's book life autonomously writes overtop of the writer's will: life as author.

Out my window crows patrol the street, under and around the parked cars, like little cadets. I wonder if what we need is less art—less artifice—and more witness to what already is.

More attention.

The details of a scene are facts—wind blowing, leaves coming loose—while the meaning we come to about the scene is just a story.

The Artist says taking notes is a way of shielding yourself from beauty. He carries only a scrap of paper, on which every now and then he records a word, a phrase at the most, with a golf pencil, in a hand so light the notations almost don't exist.

One of my problems is that I'm drawn to minutiae, to orphan images, to quotes floating out of context, to archiving little moments and fragments in my notebook that seem to add up to nothing.

Given the choice, I would rather talk to people, watch, note-take, listen, stay open, keep myself blank.

I would rather smash my canvas than invent or imagine a detail. (Cézanne)

No maps, no calculations, no hierarchy, no single point.

God made me a creature very like (a) a storm drain, (b) snow, (c) a tapeworm? Please place your answer in a sock and bury it next spring.

When I was a little boy, says the Old Blind Man, I had a kakemono from Japan. It was a picture of a hermit in a little house up a steep ravine— sacred Nature. But I rolled it up and the bugs got into it, the moths ate it.

All this time I guess I've been working from an inefficient model, asking, What does inefficiency yield? In what ways is the inefficient gesture rich and complex?

Bonnard preferred to layer pigments on top of each other as "metaphors for sensation" and often worked these layers of paint up over many years. His process was slow, gradual, considered. He worked on several canvases at once and "never felt comfortable closing a picture—there was always some slight revision that prolonged the process." Picasso found Bonnard's approach anathema and on many occasions slammed him publicly: "That's not painting what he does."

Consider that it takes two whole pages to cross the entryway of the Spouter-Inn. Melville allows himself every dalliance: the painting on the wall, the clubs and spears decorated with teeth and hair, and the rusted whaling tools. The writer seems unconcerned about getting to sea, getting to Moby-Dick, getting to the supposed crisis of the novel.

For Galen the male semen is both the "efficient cause" and the "material cause" of the embryo.

We who tend to prolong things esteem those who can speak and write succinctly, but why does it never work the other way around?

Some say Cézanne waited up to twenty minutes between brushstrokes (now, try to pause and just imagine that).

Cyril Connolly writes that he prefers autumn's fallen leaves to spring's daffodils. Connolly says spring is a "call to action"—action that will end in disillusion.

Elizabeth Bishop had a rare Picasso etching of *The Frugal Repast*, but when she lived in Brazil it grew a fungus, which a restorationist then spent years trying to remove. Both Picasso and this fungus were efficacious, though to what end?

The Sigh

The more time passes, the less the Old Blind Man discusses his sculpture. He has come to feel that no one gives a damn about it, that it is not important after all, that he will not become immortal through it.

To elevate his spirits, I try to argue the opposite. I remind him that his sculpture is visible from the interstate and that many curious travelers have exited the highway and followed the snaking road up past the rail line to his property, deserted their cars, and explored the mysterious monument, even photographed it. Some of these travelers post about his sculpture on the internet and even "rate the attraction" on a scale of 1 to 5 (of course I only read the favorable reviews to him, not the ones that call his sculpture "random" or "bizarre" or a "waste of time").

For a moment the Old Blind Man perks up, just imagining an audience of strangers inspired by his tribute to the desert—drawn to it. This may be the closest he's ever come to inhabiting the role of the artist, to feeling his aesthetic as a force in the world.

By the time I come back to visit a few days later, though, the charge has fizzled out, and the Old Blind Man is bitter again. He feels unappreciated and unacknowledged. What a waste of money, he curses.

Woman with a Crow

The other night I dreamed that women could take their eggs somewhere every month and deposit them in an environmentally safe way. At the last moment, you could examine them, before they went into the "green" hatch, but I refused to look at mine, afraid that at my age they were dry and diseased.

In Lee Krasner's *Shattered Light*, she has combined pieces of her torn-up drawings with paint that "resembles shards." Egg forms appear throughout, both whole and broken.

"Nothing is really useless," says Man Ray. "You can always find a use for even the most extravagant object."

A crow flies toward me carrying what appears to be a bloody sanitary napkin, lands on a tree limb, and begins devouring it.

I have always admired that hoarder and amateur photographer Vivian Maier shot thousands of rolls of pictures of the inside of garbage cans, which she never developed.

Later, the moon sat bright and dumpy.

In a lot of ways, I resemble my mother. I have her excellent memory, her tendency to dally around the point, her butterfly nature. This personality bouquet predisposes me to distraction and sometimes failure, but I've realized that in Art, you can take a quality that no one wants—say, inefficiency or self-doubt—and cocoon it.

You still might fail, but at least you have a place to live.

The first time someone gave Georgia O'Keeffe an alligator pear, she saved it for so long it turned into a hard, brown rattle—she could hear the seed inside. "I kept it for years—a dry thing, a wonderful shape."

Two Old People

In the University District, two middle-aged women with bleached hair chat in front of Starbucks. The 103-year-old guy who makes his daily rounds in a baby-blue suit approaches them, tipping his hat. We usually see you at the bar, one of the women says, in her raspy smoker's voice. The man smiles and stands back from them a little, and then says in a dead serious tone, You two are a coupla bombshells . . . They laugh, which sends them both coughing. We're old, they giggle. He continues looking over them like canvases on a wall.

The beauty of Bonnard's *Wild Flowers* lies in its heavy horizontals, the stems bowing to gravity.

After the flowers are done, the rain beats their brown dregs off the trees.

I do not care for people: and the idea of fame, of being a success—that's nothing, less than nothing. (Katherine Mansfield's *Journal*)

Maybe none of it matters—not integrity, not pain, not success.

The piano teacher is an older woman from Europe, a former ballet dancer and contortionist, now divorced and living alone. Her early career has rendered her disabled in her early seventies. She totters downhill toward the grocery store, clinging to a rolling shopping cart, still chain-smoking in an ultra-European way.

Giacometti: I always feel there is a fragility in living creatures, as if, at every moment, they require incredible drive just to remain standing, always at the risk of collapsing.

We think humiliation is the worst thing in the world, but it just means to bring you to earth, to *humus*.

Birds in a Cage

In a book called *How They Decorated*, I read that eccentric designer Elsa Schiaparelli loved birdcages: she kept two at home containing pigeons; an oversized cage lived at her perfume store in Paris; she designed high-fashion wire mesh coats inspired by the shape and material; and Picasso's *Oiseaux dans une cage* was her favorite painting.

"All were outward signs," says the author, "of her philosophy of transcendence through fashion."

But, may I ask, transcendence of what? The self? Homeliness? Death?

Woman Squatting with Child

In an interview with Mary Gaitskill, she discusses a movie written by Diablo Cody called *Tully*, about a woman who becomes miserable after giving birth for the first time. The film refuses to sugarcoat motherhood, portraying it as abhorrent.

The season of rebirth can become the season of unbearable anguish and grief.

Hejinian: The pair of ancient, stunted apricot trees yielded ancient, stunted apricots.

Gaitskill says it disturbed her to learn that the public was up in arms about *Tully*. They're upset that the film doesn't end with the mother character seeking psychiatric help, she explains. They want a correct and moral conclusion.

"I wanted children. I wanted to fulfill myself," says Genevieve, a character in one of Joy Williams's dark short stories: "One can never fulfill oneself."

At a literary conference, Lucia Perillo reads a poem from *Inseminating the Elephant* about a quadriplegic woman who gave birth two times "just to make her body do one thing . . . [it] could still remember." Perillo herself reads to the audience from a large, impersonal stage, where she sits in a wheelchair outfitted with a headlamp. The image in the poem and in life rebound in a tragic way.

No friend has admitted to me the hope that having her own child would relieve an awful sense of impotence and void.

I dreamed that I gave birth. I didn't see the birth, just the ugly infant with its matted, strawberry blond hair. They were about to bring the poor thing over to me and call everyone in, when I begged them to stop—I didn't want people to think I assumed they cared.

A *cloaca* is a single hole through which birds, reptiles, amphibians (and a few mammals) do all their excreting: through this single vent, they defecate, urinate, and give birth. The innovative ancient Roman sewer system was also called the Cloaca (meaning in Latin, the "public sewer, drain").

At an installation overseen by Judy Chicago, female performers made a line and simulated giving birth together. The woman at the back of the line played the role of the baby pushed through a row of thighs and eventually expelled. After pushing out three babies this way, the birthers began to rock and pet and sing to them. Some audiences were rapt; others seemed awkward, avoidant.

The Old Blind Man's Meal

I visited the Old Blind Man today at his new group home and held a straw between his lips so that he could suck fruit juice from a plastic cup. As he drank, I watched the iris of his right eye rest off to the side.

An old Croatian woman once told me that in her country, after the babies wean, they go straight to coffee and wine. When she moved to the States and saw all the children drinking milk, she became horrified. Are they sick? she asked.

Says the little girl: I'm thirsty as a man.

At the sound of the caregiver's voice, the Old Blind Man opens his mouth to get fed, like a bird. It's Pavlovian. This caregiver—the sweet one, with one side of her head braided, the braids woven through with brown, suede ribbons—doesn't seem to mind the Old Blind Man's treatment of her as a food dispensary. She laughs, gently closes his mouth, pets his hair.

Hejinian: Leave as may be, return as I should, but with the beggar baby.

Where the Old Blind Man has had a tooth extracted, someone will have to go up in the hole with a syringe of salt water.

The new baby looks like my friend at the corners of her mouth. I have morbid moments, my friend confesses, when I realize that all the baby has to survive is that sucker mouth.

Seated Old Man

At the Cloisters our tour group stops at a wooden sculpture of the Madonna and Child called *Throne of Wisdom*. This brightly painted piece depicts Christ sitting on the Virgin's lap: "The Virgin herself serves as a throne for the Christ Child," explains our docent. The two figures are stiff, without emotion. The Christ Child has a receding hairline.

Was Picasso's last lover, as some have said, more like a stultifying mother than a romantic partner? Was she a suffocator? Was she obsessed and hyperprotective? Was the painter's relationship with Jacqueline based on love or simply caregiving?

Picasso took to calling her "Maman" (supposedly, she looked more like his mother than any of the other women). He preferred that she be the one to give him his bath.

In 1965 Picasso secretly had surgery on his gallbladder and his prostate. It was the end of sex for him. He didn't paint for a year, showed few people the scar. He called that operation "the goring."

He was also losing his hearing and his eyesight, and he gave up smoking, but he began making work again at a clip, often painting twenty versions of one subject, signing and dating each version with the month, day, and year. He overflowed their enormous home studio with so much new art that they moved to a new estate—in part, he wanted the empty rooms.

Regarding the work itself, John Berger wrote: "The horror of it all is that it is a life without reality. Picasso is only happy when working. Yet, he has nothing of his own to work on. He takes up the theme of other painters' pictures . . . he decorates pots and plates that other men make for him. He is reduced to playing like a child. He becomes again the child prodigy."

Woman in a Hat with Pom-Poms
and a Printed Blouse

Picasso painted Jacqueline in dozens of flamboyant hats, in kerchiefs, turbans, and Spanish veils.

According to an old unabridged dictionary from the 1940s, the first definition of *muse* is a place or a fence or a gate where the hare slips through, derived from a word meaning "to hide."

Is the muse simply that which the trickster-artist hides behind for a while?

Well that passed the time.
It would have passed in any case. (Beckett)

No one can hoard time.

We say time is money, never money is time. Time is fixed.

Now that the Old Blind Man is bedridden and can no longer go to the Greek restaurant, he lies there asking, When you leave me, what do I do? He doesn't mean he'll be lonely when I go. He's simply wondering what is the next step in his routine. I hate to remind him that there's no routine but to lie there.

Amuse yourself. Count the sailors' pom-poms. (*Cléo from 5 to 7*)

Poet Claudia Rankine asks why people believe the imagination is unlimited—Why wouldn't the imagination be as hindered by limitation as we are in life?

Woman with a Bonnet

The yoga teacher explains reincarnation like this: We wear our bodies like an outfit. We wear and wear that outfit, which is our body, our skin. Eventually, it gets stained and torn and bedraggled. Then, finally, we change it out for a new one. "It makes sense, right?" says the teacher, cocking her topknot.

Nude with Dripping Hair

During bathtub talk the girl's arms look longer than I remember. Her knees are filthy as usual but with long, wandering legs.

She confesses she had a dream that she and a friend were going through a series of tests, which they understood to be puberty. Everyone in the dream was gray—they were shades, like in the Greek myths—and they were all naked. They had to walk through fire, swim in a pool with biting fish, have sex with the person next to them, open and read books on fire.

Listening to the girl, I'm struck that puberty and sex are a psychic burden on children—one that continues. Though of course I don't tell her this. I don't mention what will surely come (lost childhood, pimples, menarche, betrayal, existential woe, the godless void). Instead, as if the moment were choreographed, the girl finishes retelling the dream, takes a deep breath, plugs her nose, and slips completely underwater.

Woman Pissing

I used to know a large-breasted hipster who went from working as a server in a restaurant to working as a self-employed dominatrix, and later as an escort. She lived in the neighborhood and walked around in tiny vintage shorts.

In conversation she was opinionated, but not outside the norm. She talked a lot, sort of self-consciously, obsessing over her diet, but in a way that related to health concerns. Once I ran into her at a play. She was there alone. Another time I saw her out on a date on a summer night. She was not what you're picturing. She was almost plain, missable. She was a person with a vision for how the body could be used, not wasted.

When the dominatrix moved away, in search of a city in which to grow her latest business, she staged the most meticulous yard sale, with little handmade tags and all the items organized and posed in sections, like in a real boutique. She had impeccable taste, a real eye for vintage clothing. It was hard to imagine her urinating on people's faces.

At the time, farmers markets were all the rage, and she seemed like the type of person that might have made her own yogurt and bread because it's cheaper and you eliminate the packaging—the type that might even slaughter a pig if she was going to eat it. It's not clear to what degree this neighbor's professional arc correlated to a sort of trendiness, a DIY aesthetic that challenged the culture to "use all the parts of the animal."

Blue Nude

When Marguerite Duras writes in *The Lover* that "the shapes of men's bodies are miserly, internalized," and they do not "spoil like those of such girls as Hélène Lagonelle, which never last, a summer or so perhaps, that's all," she has articulated or rearticulated the central thesis of the book: absolutely nothing lasts. Beauty doesn't last, but neither does pain.

Still Life with Skull

There is a bedsore on the Old Blind Man's coccyx, which is why they flip him every two hours. Someone has taped to the wall a "turning schedule" written in magic marker.

The Riddle of the Sphinx is wrong. At the end of his life, a man doesn't go on threes, with a cane.

Me: What makes you happy now?
Old Blind Man: I don't have to publish or perish; I can just perish.

The caregivers turn the Old Blind Man onto his right side and make a mark on the flipping schedule. "I feel better," he says, facing the wall now, "but it's so temporary."

One of the challenges of aging must be to accept that much of what you learned has or will become obsolete.

Pity the cherry tree blooming over the honey bucket.

Late in life Cézanne said he was as good as dead, that nothing was left of him except to "sing small."

The Old Blind Man has become a weight that other people lift and move around. "You're light as a feather," remarks one woman, and I hear in that almost a compliment.

The Tibetan monk wonders whether life isn't a process of a question mark becoming a period. At first the question is full of longing.

I live in this bed, don't I now, says the Old Blind Man. And I don't go anywhere. And that's my life. And what am I crying or sad about? I'm doing so well.

To make a legit bouquet, the individual flowers and fronds and grasses should disappear into a larger sense of abundance. This isn't so of an arrangement, which can look sparse and lonely.

Spring moves toward death like a colorful parade.

I sit at the Old Blind Man's bed, staring at his profile, finally understanding the nineteenth-century compulsion for making life masks and death masks, like they did for Napoleon, Keats, etc.—the comfort I take in his hook nose.

This morning the little toy-like birds with yellow faces jostle loose the last of the cherry tree's petals.

In the poem "That's Where I'm Going," Clarice Lispector writes, "To my poor name is where I am going."

I think the Old Blind Man can tolerate his diaper because he cannot see it and doesn't exactly know what it is. Rather he calls it "that thing they wrap around my penis." Or he calls it a "container." Sometimes when language vanishes we can finally live.

I planned nothing, says the painter. I just allowed the pinks, oranges, and reds to cluster.

Thor tells me about how the old Jewish woman emigrated from Russia as a child, packed in a crate, straw covering her head the whole way, so the Bolsheviks wouldn't take her. And then a few years ago, at her funeral, which was held outside, how the yarmulkes kept blowing off everyone's heads, in the wind. It strikes me that the two stories describe opposite actions—the tension of life, the freedom of death.

Spring isn't about the flowers but the improbability of life after winter.

Death of Nature

During the final year of his life, Pollock drank heavily and grew unproductive. In 1956, while driving with his young mistress, he crashed the car and was killed.

Krasner painted *Birth* not long after. The eyes in Krasner's *Birth* contrast the apotropaic eyeballs in Pollock's *Birth*, 1941. Krasner's are pink and drippy yet contained by black, cloisonné lines. They are more feminine, less foreboding.

"My painting is so autobiographical," Krasner said, "if anybody can take the time to read it."

In the early seventies, some feminist artists tried to identify female characteristics or a female essence in art, a gesture that Georgia O'Keeffe had always resented and rejected. In fact, many women pushed back against the idea of an "ahistorical and transcultural female consciousness," but here is Lucy Lippard's attempt (which feels oddly beautiful and resonant with some of Krasner's later paintings, like *Gaia*, with its sweeping purples and pinks):

"A uniform density, an overall texture, often repetitive to the point of obsession; the preponderance of circular forms and central focus . . . layers or strata; an indefinable looseness or flexibility of handling; a new fondness for the pinks and pastels and the ephemeral cloud-colors that used to be taboo."

And yet, what I really want to see are Krasner's secret gray pictures from the forties. Paintings that no art movement will ever claim, that no museum or gallery or history book will ever show.

Lee Krasner, *Gray Slab*, 1942
Lee Krasner, *Gray Buildup*, 1942
Lee Krasner, *Gray Clog*, 1942
Lee Krasner, *Gray Paste*, 1943
Lee Krasner, *Gray Clay*, 1943
Lee Krasner, *Thick Gray*, 1943
Lee Krasner, *Tense Gray*, 1943
Lee Krasner, *Gray Body*, 1944
Lee Krasner, *Gray Slab*, 1944
Lee Krasner, *Gray Slab*, 1944
Lee Krasner, *Dull Gray*, 1945
Lee Krasner, *Gray Rust*, 1945
Lee Krasner, *Gray Leak*, 1945
Lee Krasner, *Gray Pus*, 1945
Lee Krasner, *Gray Increase*, 1945
Lee Krasner, *Old Gray*, 1945
Lee Krasner, *Gray Mass*, 1946
Lee Krasner, *Gray Crust*, 1946
Lee Krasner, *Dry Gray*, 1946
Lee Krasner, *Gray Slab*, 1946
Lee Krasner, *Gray Slab*, 1946

Gray is not a negative color.

Last Moments

Alberto Giacometti devoted his career to "making resemblances," but near the end of life decided the gap between art and reality was too wide; he finally accepted that he would never solve the problem: "I could spend the rest of my life copying a chair," he sighed (though I suspect he knew instinctively that his life's work was insoluble, and took some odd pleasure in the difficulty of his task).

Marina Abramović claims that Giacometti has survived because he was not doing anything trendy at the time—he was sculpting people's souls.

Painting a gray sky but then adding new colors—a touch of purple, then touch of pink, etc.

Cézanne would lay out the elements of a still life (say, a pot of primroses and several apples) and rearrange them hundreds of times until they were just right. It then might take hundreds of sessions to finish a painting. He rarely used fresh flowers because he couldn't keep up with them—they would wilt before the end.

"Will I reach the goal I've sought so long and hard?" wrote Cézanne a few days before his death. "I'm still studying nature and it seems to me that I'm making slow progress."

Come May the hellish tulip falls open, one blade flopped forward like a glam rocker licking the air.

When Rachmaninoff got old, says the Old Blind Man, he didn't want to stretch his fingers out to hear the chords he loved anymore.

Barista says of the album playing in the cafe, I liked this, but only for about ten listens.

Bonnard executed his very last still life in 1946—your standard bowl of fruit on a table. The fruit in this bowl is extremely rotten yet rendered in such a painterly way that it charms you. After a lifetime everything Bonnard knows about painting works to make the green mold on the peach as rich and putrid as possible.

When in doubt, cross it out, says the Artist. He finds that the things you doubt just get worse and worse. My response would be, Don't the things you don't doubt also get worse and worse?

He speaks of the ease of writing in a new form. Why would he be interested in his ease?

Hejinian: Slowly, to no outcome.

Cézanne told his mother that finishing things was a goal for imbeciles.

The failing Asian restaurant became a failing French restaurant.

The Old Blind Man and I read on Wikipedia that Paul Valéry was buried in the seaside cemetery next to the Mediterranean featured in his poem "Graveyard by the Sea." This thrills the Old Blind Man—to think that the poet would end up back in the poem, in what Valéry called the "Temple of Time." Yet among the living, says the Old Blind Man, Valéry is "completely forgotten."

When you think of life in seasons, we won't see that many springs.

David Markson's antinovels published at the end of his life wrestle with the question of whether any artist or piece of art is immortal. We've only embraced Shakespeare for twenty generations—the books seem to argue—which is nothing compared to eternity!

Carole Maso: Life doesn't last, art doesn't last.

Everything goes, says the Old Blind Man; everything you keep has to be disposed of.

The Artist took his daughter for a walk down the beach. They came back with rocks, a crab shell, and a plastic butterfly. At dinner we examined the crab shell—the crab still in it, with one stiff white eye intact.

The design on the shell was orange and white and resembled a painstakingly composed mosaic, or as Sylvia Plath once described such a shell in one of her poems, "A samurai death mask done / on a tiger tooth, less for / Art's sake than God's." Studying the etched lines, the girl said, Maybe when we die we become an imprint. Maybe our portrait appears on a shell or leaf, or in an animal's skin.

In my opinion this would be reincarnation at its finest—to come back to life as a detail.

Woman Seated in a Garden

At Twenty-First and Valencia, I photograph a window installation. Paper flowers of various sizes dance in the window. On a piece of masking tape someone has written, "The flower is the beginning and the ending."

A couple passes as I'm snapping the photograph. The woman says, "Those flowers look like meat."

My professor explains that as a writer he wants the thinnest possible membrane between art and life. Sometimes mine is so dangerously thin that it's not art at all, just a deep, off-page investigation of patterns, a tracking of sensations, repetitions.

After a near-fatal surgery for duodenal cancer, Matisse spent his late years in bed or wheelchair-bound, working with paper and scissors instead of canvas and brush. An assistant would paint white paper with colorful gouache and then hold it up for him.

From his wheelchair he cut a menagerie of shapes into the paper she held up: circles and feathers and diamonds and rectangles and seeds and sharks and birds and jellyfish and leaves and triangles. Then he would instruct her to pin these shapes to the wall in various configurations: "I have made a little garden all around me where I can walk," Matisse said. "There are leaves, fruits, a bird."

Until death Matisse tinkered with many of the compositions: "Forms were pinned into one grouping and then removed to join another; works were composed in one orientation and then rotated or inverted. The many visible pinholes attest to this state of flux" (museum placard, MOMA).

After his death existing compositions were considered final. But for Matisse the process was inherently provisional, dynamic.

The least decisive people I know are cautious and make few decisions. The most decisive make decisions rapidly, and lots in succession, but I don't think decisive people have some special purchase on being human. One choice often reverses the effects of a previous choice.

Beckett: My soul is restless. Both my souls are restless.

Krasner began *Pollination* in the fifties, laying down the red and green organic forms, and then abandoned the painting. In the sixties she came back to the canvas with a different style, a harder touch. With the edge of a brush, she carved crisp, white forms into the soft red and green blooms, interspersing styles from two periods of her life.

What is the relationship between certainty and a pin?

A few years ago, when the MOMA exhibited Matisse's cutouts, my dad remembered a story from *Sports Illustrated* about a Siberian orthopedist. This doctor had discovered an important surgery while taking care of wounded soldiers: After cutting out the infected area in a soldier's leg, he would insert a metal bicycle part from scraps lying around. Then the body would send copious blood into that region to fight off the invasive object, killing bad bacteria. This influx resurged the infected area with new life.

Thinking about revisions and pins, I realize that I find it even freer and more creative to *look* at art than to make it—there is a ranginess and an unfinished quality to that process. One is called upon to complete the picture but not cordon off the relationship.

Seeing can always open up again.

Woman in a Shawl

All this effort for an imperfect book.

What is a book anyways but notes in fancy clothes.

"My dream is to finish my book," wrote Jean Rhys at age seventy, still toiling away at *Wide Sargasso Sea*, "get a face lift and a bright red wig. Also a lovely fur coat. Underneath I will wear a purple dress and ropes of pearls. Or what do you say to rags?"

Yet another theory came to me. I was thinking about the way my artistic process resembles a cultured pearl growing very angstily around an alien nucleus, a grafted bead, an itch.

Possible change of title: "Ugly Pearls."

Possible addition of a section in the appendix: "Table of Mixed Metaphors."

I don't necessarily look forward to writing any more than I used to—the endless decision-making still overwhelms me—but lately I enjoy the routine. Wrapped in blankets, looking out the window, musing, feeling the light shift as the clouds move.

I don't feel so sinful this day as I did, because I have written something and the tide is still high. The ancient landmarks are covered. Ah! But to write better! Let me write better, more deeply, more largely. (from Katherine Mansfield's *Journal*)

Near the Methodist church, someone is running and raving, "I am a willing vessel!"

Whereas the Artist wants every scene to opine, I've decided it's okay for the text to feel embryonic, locked.

It's okay to approach the world softly, curiously—just to be a woman sitting by a window.

I am not interested in constructing a building, so much as in having a perspicuous view of the foundations of possible buildings. (Ludwig Wittgenstein)

James Turrell's Roden Crater is decades in the making: the journey to it is part of the art. (Though Australian artist Andrew Rogers tells the *Washington Post* that we shouldn't consider Turrell a bona fide land artist if he has yet to complete one sculpture.)

Oh, to remain a draft, to remain unwritten—simply felt and simply hoped for!

I wonder what all these thoughts would look like as a clay pot, or a dance.

The wonderful micropenis sculpture of Giacometti.

Why are you sure of yourself? she asks.
I'm sure and unsure, he says, but I hide the pangs of insecurity with overconfidence.

G. K. Chesterton reminds us in "The Fallacy of Success" that success in and of itself is not something you strive toward: a donkey is successful in being a donkey.

"We succeeded at being born," says photographer Isaac Layman, "and we are going to succeed at death. We're going to three-pointer death from mid-court."

At an abysmal comedy show, emceed by an ugly drag queen with pretty knees, waxy blond wig, short dress, fake pearls, I listen mostly to the coordinating conjunctions—but, also, so—and the transitions between jokes.

All my life I worked hard at an immaterial calling and died a pauper, ecstatic with philosophies.

Looking without shaping.

Lots of small effort, no grand thing.

La joie de vivre (Pastorale)

Legend has it that Kees van Dongen took the train from Rotterdam to Paris and then tore up his return ticket. The painter installed himself in the studio where Picasso was working and eventually found his own personal style, characterized by the use of garish colors. He painted the cafés, the clowns, and the prostitutes—one Anita, her legs open, body accessorized in just a pink, fluttering garter.

From Paris he traveled to smaller towns with an easel, hoping to encounter as much humanity as possible. He claimed he had a physical feeling for people and didn't bother trying to portray space or light in a new way, or even the person *behind* the person.

He painted sailors and tarts at port, in fiery pinks and sad grays and paisley. He dealt with outward appearances—he felt that appearances were stunning enough, that life was more beautiful than a portrait of life.

Does a person who spends all day inside painting an apple love the world? he asked.

Still Life with Fruit

Even my mother wonders why I don't give the writing up, move along. She suggests speaking to a creativity counselor who specializes in helping artists through blocks, helping them find their inner child.

A piece of art that never tired of life—what would that look like?

Idiosyncratic sculptor Andrea Zittel says she's interested in the way we try to fashion our own utopias—and how even these utopias cycle through and cover over each other, the rococo giving way to the modern. Zittel says it takes at least ten years for people to understand her work.

Krasner: All my work keeps going like a pendulum.

I know this is a chaotic book, a flawed book. I just wanted to make something rich, vibrant, and reflective of how life feels to me.

"Weak, formless, and imperfect."

I'm still trying to invent a form that accepts aesthetic decisions as provisional, events as uncertain, life as unportrayable—a form that concedes that art is unsatisfying.

Waiting for the apple blossoms to disappear into the leaves, for the book to finish itself.

Waiting

According to her translator, Clarice Lispector wrote her most canonical stories in the 1960s (i.e., *Family Ties*). Later in her life, she really pared the language down. The stories got very campy, burlesque, as if she didn't care about her literary reputation anymore.

Does art interest me mostly as a response, a human behavior? Yes, maybe so. That's probably why I never had much interest in the scientific principles behind visual art—the electromagnetic spectrum, the golden ratio, and all that.

Paulus Berensohn, a modern dancer who in the 1950s embarked on a second career as a potter, said as he aged he cared about a "behavior of art," not achievement or a product. What interested him was that all human beings are creative.

Fruit trees of every kind on earth that bear fruit with the seed in it.

In her frail old age, often dressed in a black cape and signature gaucho hat, Georgia O'Keeffe lived in a traditional Abiquiú house in New Mexico and learned to sculpt with clay. She performed a sort of free fall toward death through her embrace of a dry world.

Woman Reading

A few years ago at the Greek restaurant, the Old Blind Man wanted to know what colors I was wearing. It was not kinky, I don't think, but a nasty attempt at personality analysis. Black, white, and gray, I said, looking at my outfit. Well, he said, that's rather subdued.

I was reading him a biographical sketch of the French artist Gaudier-Brzeska, who died at twenty-three, fighting in the trenches during World War I. He, too, struggled with the value of art and eventually gave up drawing: "The more I go into the woods and the fields the more distrustful I become of art and wish all civilization to the devil."

Are you paying attention? I asked the Old Blind Man.

Like a seagull, he said.

What do you mean, like a seagull?

You're dressed like a seagull, he said.

Maybe, I said.

I saw myself as an enormous seagull sitting on a huge egg that had no intention of hatching, just kept getting bigger underneath me. I told the Old Blind Man my vision.

A stone, he said.

A stone?

It could be a stone and not an egg.

Maybe you're right, I said.

I imagined passing a gigantic stone, something like Gaudier-Brzeska's phallic sculpture, *Head of Ezra Pound*.

The daydream was so vivid that I squirmed a bit in my chair. Isn't passing a stone also a kind of birth, I thought to myself.

When we went back to the biography, Gaudier-Brzeska was in the process of making a hundred preparatory drawings for Pound's head, most of which have since been lost. I thought it was an interesting story, but the Old Blind Man still seemed distracted.

Are you paying attention? I asked again.

Well, of course, he said dryly, I'm hanging on every word.

Woman Throwing a Stone

At a party full of writers, I overhear someone complaining about the book he's reading. How painful it is watching it "try to finish itself." It's embarrassing, he says. And he's right, someday we should stop doing it. Maybe just walk away.

Kiki Smith's sculpture, *Pee Body*, seems vulgar from one angle and quiet and elegant from another. Smith carved a woman out of beeswax. The figure squats on the floor of Harvard's art museum, head bowed over her legs. There is an overwhelming feeling of despair. Why? Behind her trails a whole sea of urine composed of yellow glass pearls.

Smith: I always think the whole history of the world is in your body.

How ingenious that a sculpture, a painting, has no end and no beginning, unlike a book. A book is at the mercy of time.

I wish this book could end a hundred ways, every last word diverging into the next. I would end with the veins of a leaf, which would become the veins of my mother's tongue, which would become an argument the Artist and I had about endings, which would become Picasso's painting of a woman throwing a stone, which would become a carved figurine from ancient Spain scratched with little markings we can no longer interpret.

Woman at the Window

Maybe the problem is that I hang on every word. Look at me, still hanging on to all these little scribbles.

A vine clinging to the face of a wall, a bougainvillea braiding itself without judgment to even the ugliest house or rusted gate.

In a painting by Andrea Belvedere, the blue morning glory twists around a dead branch. To be alive is cloying.

Or maybe that's not right.

Maybe I can't hang on at all.

And maybe nothing hangs on.

Nothing stays or keeps.

Possible change of title: "Clouds Drift, etc."

Acknowledgments

Thank you to *Exacting Clam* for publishing the discarded epigraphs (which appeared as "Epigraphs for an Abandoned Novel") in their inaugural issue, and to Hawthorne Books for printing the diagrams in *Life Is Short—Art Is Shorter: In Praise of Brevity* (2015).

Many thanks to 360 Xochi Quetzal and Ragdale Foundation, two idyllic artist residencies where I spent weeks drawing maps of books I would have liked to write.

I'm indebted to Courtney Ochsner and University of Nebraska Press for publishing the current draft of this manuscript—and freeing me from it.

Melville: This whole book is but a draught—nay, but the draught of a draught.

There are many people I've tormented over the years while struggling my way through this project, especially David Shields. I'm so grateful to you, David, for your ongoing mentorship, for the persistence you model, and for your patience with "Impasse." Also, of course, to my loving family, and to Jess, Sarah Erickson, and my Weird Sisters.

Katharine Adams Ogle, you donated hopeful charms—drawing pads, felt-tip markers, giant Post-its, erasers—and a muse.

Thank you to Richard Kenney for lessons and riddles about language that I return to, like mantras.

Most of all, I must acknowledge how much I tortured Thomas Walton during the making and unmaking and making and unmaking of this book. Thomas, thank you for your sense of humor, partnership, wit, grace, and for the ways you challenge me. Grace for the great, grace for the rogues! You don't like compliments, platitudes, or list poems, so I'll stop there.

Appendix

Discarded Epigraphs

Writing is hot and it hurts and it doesn't make me happy.

—LUCIE BROCK-BROIDO

There are times when I could be physically sick, the stuff's so low.

—FLAUBERT, WHILE COMPOSING *MADAME BOVARY*

He declared that his imagination was hidebound; it was there, but it pulled hard. After he got a notion for a story, months passed before he could get any sort of personal contract with it, or feel any potency to handle it.

—WILLA CATHER ON STEPHEN CRANE

I have not yet made something that TOTALLY pleases me.

—VIJA CELMINS

Even in my brain, in my head, I can think and act and write wonders—wonders; but the moment I really try to put them down I fail miserably.

—KATHERINE MANSFIELD

Think of something . . . Have an idea. A bright idea.

—BECKETT

Spoken in the voice of the Sun: "a cloud intervening . . . / would be stronger than I and I be discredited."

—MARIANNE MOORE

All these people are making their mark in the world,
While I, pigheaded, awkward,
Different from the rest,
Am only a glorious infant still nursing at the breast.

—LAO TZU

Therefore, I am not a necessary being.

—BLAISE PASCAL

Yesterday was my Birth Day. So completely has a whole year passed, with scarcely the fruits of a *month.*—O Sorrow and Shame . . . I have done nothing!

—SAMUEL TAYLOR COLERIDGE

He had been trying to live and think in a way that he hoped would end by making a poet of him, but it hadn't worked.

—KATHERINE ANNE PORTER

No man but a blockhead ever wrote except for money.

—SAMUEL JOHNSON

I have not written anything today worth a sou.

—KATHERINE MANSFIELD

The more books we read, the clearer it becomes that the true function of a writer is to produce a masterpiece and that no other task is of any consequence. Obvious though it should be, how few writers will admit it, or having drawn the conclusion, will be prepared to lay aside the piece of iridescent mediocrity on which they have embarked!

—CYRIL CONNOLLY, *THE UNQUIET GRAVE*

Almost every man wastes part of his life attempting to display qualities which he doesn't possess.

—JOHNSON

I am but a link in the chain of heretics and failures, a woodwind solo in the interminable symphony.

—CONNOLLY

I am irritated by my own writing. I am like a violinist whose ear is true, but whose fingers refuse to reproduce precisely the sounds he hears.

—FLAUBERT

Nothing but wretchedness and error come from me.

—PASCAL

I am posing here as a lady with a weak heart and lungs of Spanish leather.

—MANSFIELD

Thou art infected.

—SHAKESPEARE, *THE TEMPEST*

To enter your own mind you need to be armed to the teeth.

—PAUL VALÉRY

August 30th: Morning tears return; spirits at their lowest ebb. Approaching forty, sense of total failure: not a writer but a ham actor whose performance is clotted with egotism; dust and ashes.

—AGAIN CONNOLLY, MY MELANCHOLY FRIEND

Aristotle writes that you'll suffer over the mysteries but will learn nothing new.

—BRENDA HILLMAN

So far I haven't succeeded. I might not even be a sculptor at all. I feel I don't understand volumes.

—ALBERTO GIACOMETTI

Seems like my life has erectile dysfunction.

—MIRA GONZALEZ

Had I followed my pleasure and chosen what I plainly have a decided talent for: police spy, I should have been happier than I afterwards became.

—KIERKEGAARD

I hope this preamble will soon come to an end.

—BECKETT

Voices

Rae Armantrout, "Write Home," in *Up to Speed*

Julian Barnes, *Keeping an Eye Open: Essays on Art*

Samuel Beckett, *Waiting for Godot*

Yves Bonnefoy, *Giacometti*

Lilian Brion-Guerry, "The Elusive Goal," in *Cézanne: The Late Work*, ed. William Rubin (Museum of Modern Art)

Pierre Cabanne, *Pablo Picasso: His Life and Times*

Steven Cantor and Peter Spirer, *Blood Ties: The Life and Work of Sally Mann*

Whitney Chadwick, *Women, Art, and Society*

Marc Chagall, *My Life*

John Cheever, *The Journals of John Cheever*

G. K. Chesterton, "The Fallacy of Success"

Judy Chicago, *Through the Flower: My Struggle as a Woman Artist*

Cyril Connolly, *The Unquiet Grave: A Word Cycle by Palinurus*

Katrina Dodson (on Clarice Lispector)

David Douglas Duncan, *Viva Picasso*

Marguerite Duras, *Practicalities* and *The Lover*

Suzanne Farrell (on Balanchine)

Andrew Feld (on Robert Browning's "My Last Duchess")

David W. Galenson, *Old Masters and Young Geniuses: The Two Life Cycles of Creative Geniuses*

Vivian Gornick, *The End of the Novel of Love* (quoting Jean Rhys's published letters)

Lyn Hejinian, *My Life*

Henri Matisse: The Cut-Outs, Museum of Modern Art exhibit

Robert Hobbs, *Lee Krasner* (Modern Masters Series)

Susan Howe, *My Emily Dickinson*

Robert Hughes, *Shock of the New*

Isaac Layman—Paradise, Frye Art Museum exhibit

Karen L. King, ed., *Images of the Feminine in Gnostic Schools*

April Kingsley, *The Turning Point: The Abstract Expressionists and the Transformation of American Art*

Lee Krasner, oral history interviews, November 2, 1964–April 11, 1968, and 1972, Archives of American Art, Smithsonian Institution

Gail Levin, *Lee Krasner: A Biography*

Los Angeles County Museum of Art tour, soft-spoken docent in green tartan blazer with gold buttons

Sally Mann, Nybourg Photojournalism Conference

Katherine Mansfield, *The Journal of Katherine Mansfield*, ed. J. Middleton Murry

Carole Maso, *AVA*

Peter Matthiessen and George Plimpton interview with William Styron, *Paris Review*

Mary Jo Maynes, Ann Waltner, Birgitte Soland, Ulrike Strasser, eds., *Gender, Kinship and Power: A Comparative and Interdisciplinary History*

Don McDonagh, *Martha Graham*

Metropolitan Museum of Art tour of Impressionists, fancy docent in black silk scarf and pear-cut diamonds

Michel de Montaigne, *The Complete Essays*

Marianne Moore, *Collected Poems*

Eleanor Nairne, ed., *Lee Krasner: Living Colour* (especially Katy Siegel's essay "Nothing Outside Nature")

Georgia O'Keeffe, *Georgia O'Keeffe*

Blaise Pascal, *Pensées*

John E. Pfeiffer, *The Creative Explosion: An Inquiry into the Origins of Art and Religion*

Antonio Porchia, *Voices*

Ross Posnock, *Renunciation: Acts of Abandonment by Writers, Philosophers, and Artists*

Revisiting Giacometti in His Own Words (film)

Seattle Art Museum tour, fair-haired docent for *Gauguin and Polynesia: An Elusive Paradise*

David Shields (Shakespeare's legacy is brief compared to eternity—that idea belongs to David)

Michael Silverblatt interview with Claudia Rankine, *Bookworm*

Adam Summers (on ichthyology)

P. Gaye Tapp, *How They Decorated: Inspiration from Great Women of the Twentieth Century*

Towards Impressionism: Landscape Painting from Corot to Monet, Frye Art Museum exhibit

Anne Truitt, *Day Book: The Journal of an Artist*

Chögyam Trungpa, *Dharma Art*

Vogue, "Paris after Dark," February 2012 (anecdote about Dora Maar is theirs)

Wesley Wehr, *The Accidental Collector: Art, Fossils, and Friendships*

Edmund White, *The Flâneur: A Stroll Through the Paradoxes of Paris*

CPSIA information can be obtained
at www.ICGtesting.com
Printed in the USA
LVHW100053241122
733809LV00006BA/388